Endorsements for *Fresh Ideas*

I'm forever looking for just this variety of "fresh ideas" to stimulate the creative juices it takes to keep church life exciting, contemporary and appealing. Diana has bound together a wonderful assortment of delightful helps and encouragements in this one volume.

Dr. Bobby Welch
Past President, Southern Baptist Convention
Author, Retired Pastor, FBC Daytona Beach, Florida

This ready resource is short and simple, organized for easy use, and filled with great and practical ideas for almost every occasion.

—Steve Swofford
Pastor, FBC Rockwall, Texas
President, Southern Baptists of Texas Convention

The most useful book on the nuts and bolts of "doing church" to come along in decades! This encyclopedic collection of concrete ideas is a must for all ministers and members who want to keep their church functions, ordinances, outreach, ministries, etc. innovative and effective. Get your church out of its rut with this highly usable toolbox.

—Dr. Mark Edlund
Executive Director, Colorado Baptist Convention
Denver, Colorado

Who isn't looking for *Fresh Ideas?* Diana Davis saves us much time and offers an overwhelming abundance of creativity and productivity to be applied in countless settings in the kingdom. Whether in women's ministry events, special occasions in the church, and in a myriad of ways throughout the kingdom of Christ—here you will find fuel to get your own wheels turning as well as carefully scripted ideas ready to use on a moment's notice. I have been reading the author's column in the Indiana Baptist State Paper with avid interest. Many of her columns have been clipped and filed. I welcome the opportunity to have them all bound and on my shelf for my ready reference and to share with my students!

—Dr. Dorothy Kelley Patterson
Professor of Theology in Women's Studies
Southwestern Baptist Theological Seminary
Fort Worth, Texas

. . . innovative, imaginative, and inventive . . .

—Clark Harless
Senior Pastor, Calvary Baptist Church
Knox, Indiana

This book will awaken your creative heart and mind so that many more may worship and serve Jesus Christ with vigor.

—Sid Woodruff
Men's and Deacon Ministry Specialist
LifeWay Christian Resources
Nashville, Tennessee

Fresh Ideas is a must-have book for every pastor and his wife. I plan to buy it by the case to give to pastors and association leaders.

—Dr. Craig Culbreth
Director of Partnership Missions, Florida Baptist Convention
Jacksonville, Florida

Diana Davis brings the experience of a pastor's wife, a leader, women's speaker, VBS teacher, friend, and most importantly an encourager to inspire me and others. She weaves practical application, excitement, and biblical insight through all of her articles.

—Jim Bohrer
Pastor, Hope Community Church
Brownsburg, Indiana

Once in a while a book comes along that is so jam-packed with creative, practical ideas, you want everyone in the ministry to have it. This is just such a book.

—David and Nancy Baldwin
Executive Director, Alaska Baptist Convention
Anchorage, Alaska

A priceless book for the seasoned minister as well as the beginner. Her ideas are impacting how our church planters are doing *church* even here in Kiev, Ukraine.

—Joel and Mary Ellen Ragains
IMB Missionaries
Kiev, Ukraine

Many of these ideas will be implemented in our Third-World culture as we train leaders in the harvest.

—Rich Fleming
IMB Missionary
Querétaro, Mexico

Diana Davis exudes creativity in her new book. Her joy for life and her years of experience in and around church ministry have well equipped her with a host of wonderful insights and practical ideas invaluable to any church leader. What a treasure to now have these in one volume. I highly recommend this book.

—Dr. Gary Cook
President, Dallas Baptist University
Dallas, Texas

. . . a must-have . . . buy it, use it, and give a copy to a friend.

—Connie Cavanaugh
Speaker, columnist, and author of *From Faking It to Finding Grace*
Calgary, Canada

Fresh Ideas is full of wit, humor, and practical, good-hearted advice for everyday living. This book is a wonderful tool that puts fresh air into some stuffy routines. I highly recommend it.

—Dr. Thane Barnes
Executive Director, Nevada Baptist Convention
Reno, Nevada

. . . a "stoking the fires of evangelism" book . . . cutting edge but practical ideas.

—Sandra K. (Mrs. Anthony) Payton
Pastor's Wife/Heart2Heart/Sisters Who Care Facilitator
Come As You Are Community Church
Fort Wayne, Indiana

Diana Davis's *Fresh Ideas* columns have frequently enlivened the pages of *Florida Baptist Witness* with pithy, practical, and sometimes provocative thoughts that are helpful to churches, pastors, and all followers of Christ.

—James A. Smith Sr.
Executive Editor, *Florida Baptist Witness*
Jacksonville, Florida

Diana's monthly article in the *Indiana Baptist* has encouraged church leaders across our state and now is going to make an even greater impact on the entire Christian community. I recommend every church leader read this book.

—Dr. Mark Hearn
Senior Pastor, Northside Baptist Church, Indianapolis
President, State Convention of Baptists in Indiana

Diana's fresh ideas are like a breath of fresh air. In this one book you will find the practical resources that will revitalize your church's ministry.

—Dr. David Lee
Executive Director, Baptist Convention of Maryland/Delaware
Columbia, Maryland

In a day when churches must think outside the box to see people regularly, consistently won to faith in Jesus Christ, *Fresh Ideas* is exactly what we need!

—Larry Snyder
Pastor, Victory Baptist Church
Clinton, Indiana

. . . a great resource for every Christian leader. Packed with useful ideas for all aspects of church life, this book will help you think creatively about your church's ministry.

—Ann (Mrs. Jeff) Iorg
President's Wife
Golden Gate Theological Seminary
Mill Valley, California

Fresh Ideas should be on the shelf of every church staff member and church leader.

—Marty King
Associate Executive Director, Illinois Baptist State Convention
Editor, *Illinois Baptist*
Springfield, Illinois

Diana Davis's *Fresh Ideas* have invigorated the imaginations of myself and the colaborers in our church. I highly recommend this innovative, yet easy to use, collection of practical, Spirit-filled suggestions.

—Ashley Ray
Pastor, Avon Baptist Church
Avon, Indiana

Rarely does one find purposeful answers and insights with such ease . . . an opportunity to receive help without paying a great price of precious time.

—Tim Clark
Executive Director, Utah-Idaho Baptist Convention
Draper, Utah

If you have been doing business as usual in your church planning and you need a new spark, then this book is for you. We highly recommend Diana Davis's creative, imaginative, and practical ideas.

—Jeanette and Dr. Carlisle Driggers
Executive Director, South Carolina Baptist Convention
Columbia, South Carolina

I have participated in many of these *Fresh Ideas* with Diana over the years, and I have found them extremely practical and usable.

—Paula Hearon
Wife of the Executive Director
Dallas Baptist Association
Dallas, Texas

Pastors and church leaders continually need inspirational nuggets to help stay current. Diana's insight reminds us that "little things can make a big difference."

—Dr. Charles L. Wilson
Senior Pastor, Sunnyvale First Baptist Church
Sunnyvale, Texas

Why are Diana Davis's fresh ideas so captivating and practical? . . . a mind set on Christ and a determination to find new and fresh ways, to share the wonder of God's love.

—Dr. Jimmy and Joan Barrentine
Executive Director, Iowa Baptist Convention
Des Moines, Iowa

Fresh Ideas are word pictures that demonstrate timeless truths in action.

—Dr. John Rogers Jr.
Missions and Evangelism Team Leader
State Convention of Baptists in Indiana
Indianapolis, Indiana

Diana packs more useful, practical material into a page than most do in a chapter!

—Rose Bear
Baptist Collegiate Ministry
Indiana State University
Terre Haute, Indiana

. . . creative, simple, and fun. They are ideas the entire church will enjoy doing.

—Chris Gustafson
Pastor, Eastern Heights Baptist Church
Jeffersonville, Indiana

Diana Davis skillfully offers us a plethora of tested, invigorating ideas. *Fresh Ideas* has the potential to rejuvenate the ministry of your church and become an indispensable resource for best practices!

—Bobbye (Mrs. Jerry) Rankin
International Mission Board
Wife of IMB President, Former Missionary, Asia
Richmond, Virginia

. . . a rich spiritual smorgasbord of ministry ideas that you can immediately put into practice or easily adapt . . . regardless of the size or style of your church ministry.

—Dr. Scott Miller
Senior Pastor, Graceland Baptist Church
New Albany, Indiana

This is a book every pastor will want to have in his library and will want to share with key leaders in the church. Diana's many years as a pastor's wife keep her focused on strengthening the local church and reaching out to the community.

—Dr. David Waltz
Executive Director, Baptist Convention of Pennsylvania-South Jersey
Harrisburg, Pennsylvania

You will be amazed at how many times you will read find yourself saying, "That's a fresh idea that will work in my church"!

—Jaye Copeland
Childhood and WMU/Women's Ministry
State Convention of Baptists in Indiana
Indianapolis, Indiana

Our church has used her ideas, and they have helped our people to think more creatively about ministry.

—Paul Hollis
Minister of Education, Oakhill Baptist Church
Evansville, Indiana

Fresh Ideas is more than a collection of creative thoughts! Diana Davis has taken relevancy to the next level.
Every pastor should read this book and make it available to church leaders!

—Dr. Jim Hamilton
Executive Director-Treasurer, Dakota Baptist Convention
Bismarck, North Dakota

I was personally enriched by reviewing the multiple ways of breathing fresh meaning and life into the routine elements of ministry. This book will have significant influence in helping creative thinkers think beyond the ordinary when planning the work of ministry.

—Dr. Veryl Henderson
Executive Director, Hawaii Pacific Baptist Convention
Honolulu, Hawaii

ISBN: 978-0-8054-4492-6

Published by B&H Publishing Group,
Nashville, Tennessee

Dewey Decimal Classification: 254
Subject Heading: CHURCH ADMINISTRATION \ CHURCH RENEWAL

Unless otherwise noted, all Scripture references are taken from the
Holman Christian Standard Bible® © 1999, 2000, 2002, 2003 by
Holman Bible Publishers. Other versions include: *The Message,* the New
Testament in Contemporary English, © 1993 by Eugene H. Peterson,
published by NavPress, Colorado Springs, Colo.; NLT, New Living Translation,
copyright © 1996. Used by permission of Tyndale House Publishers, Inc.,
Wheaton, IL 60189 USA. All rights reserved.; TLB, The Living Bible,
copyright © Tyndale House Publishers, Wheaton, Ill., 1971, used by
permission; and NKJV, New King James Version, copyright © 1979,
1980, 1982, Thomas Nelson, Inc., Publishers.

1 2 3 4 5 6 7 8 9 10   11 10 09 08 07

fresh ideas

1,000 ways to grow a thriving and energetic church

diana davis

Keep on shining!
Diana Davis

B&H
PUBLISHING GROUP
Nashville, Tennessee

Contents

Dedication

To Dr. Stephen P. Davis,
My husband
my best friend
my love
my greatest encourager.
Thank you for believing in me.

My son, Justin,
the most remarkable young man I know,
who between PhD work, teaching, and triathalons
still finds time to encourage his mom.

My amazing daughter, Autumn,
whose creative brain makes mine look bland,
and whose sold-out love for God shines brightly.

Keep on shining!

Acknowledgments

The old saying, "There's nothing new under the sun," fits in this circumstance. Yes, we've implemented the vast majority of ideas in this book in the churches where Steve and I have served. But you'll find versions of many of them in hundreds of other churches across our nation. Some of the ideas are totally original; some are updated with ideas observed in Indiana Baptist churches.

This book began with an accumulation of ministry ideas from decades of ministry in the local church. I'm forever indebted to the churches in Texas who allowed me the honor of being pastor's wife for over three decades. You tolerated and even encouraged all my creative energies, and God blessed our efforts.

I owe a debt of gratitude to every church, pastor, and pastor's wife in Indiana, too numerous to name here, for encouraging me, sharing ideas, and demonstrating fresh ways to share the gospel with our world. I am inspired and blessed each time I have the privilege of being in your churches.

Thanks to the Indiana Baptist state newspaper team for inviting me to write the "Fresh Ideas" columns each issue and to the other state Baptist papers and their editors who have printed them.

Special thanks to Tom Atkinson for his huge help with blogging advice, Autumn Davis for youth ministry ideas, Rose Bear for college expertise, and to Jaye Copeland, John Rogers, and Bev Olonoh for your valuable insights and input. A huge thank-you to my mom, Wanda Riddle, and sister, Nancy Schultze, for their hours of input and long-distance encouragements. To Justin and Autumn. To our wonderful pastor, Jim Bohrer. My favorite Aunt June and Uncle Ferris. And to each of you friends who have encouraged me, prodded me, and shared your own fresh ideas. I thank you all sincerely.

And most of all, I thank my adorable husband, Steve. These ideas came from our joint efforts in ministry and creativity to honor God, and I would never have written them down without his gentle persuasion.

Introduction

Simply going to church for most of my life didn't make me an expert on church freshness. Being married to a pastor for decades didn't do it either, but it certainly helped fine-tune that urge. My pastor/husband and I have had the privilege of serving in innovative, growing churches. We've had the thrill of helping start a new church, serve in a medium-sized church and in a large church. Most of the ideas in this book have been tested and proved in those settings.

But when Steve and I moved to Indiana, where he serves as executive director for the State Convention of Baptists in Indiana, we were suddenly attending several different churches every week.

And I noticed a consistent common denominator
among growing, vibrant churches of every size:
Freshness.

There should be no such thing as a stale church. We serve a life-giving, vibrant, exciting Savior. Worship in his house should be no less!

When you attend the same church for years—as you should!—you tend to think that every church does everything exactly like your church. To some extent that's true. But I quickly observed that every church has its own way of doing things—its own personality, if you will. To be honest, it's not usually big things that add freshness to a church. Small adjustments can make a world of difference.

This book is a collection of small ideas, simple things to help freshen up how your church does church. It's organized as a reference tool for church leaders, divided into seventy-five topics. Each topic offers several simple ideas, designed to squeeze your creative juices. It's a fun book, and you don't necessarily need to sit and read every page. Just browse and dream, consider and pray.

You may want to read it with a highlighter in hand, crossing off the ideas you already implement, scribbling the ones you don't like, and circling some ideas you'd like to try. No, not every idea will fit your church. Some will delight you. Some won't. Some will make you laugh hysterically. But I'm praying that at least a few ideas on these pages will reignite your fire for serving God, fit your church perfectly, and help freshen up how your church does church.

> "Bring me back from gray exile, put a fresh wind in my sails!"
> (Ps. 51:12 *The Message*)

Baptism

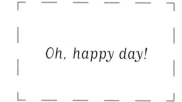
Oh, happy day!

"So those who accepted his message were baptized."

—Acts 2:41

It's more significant than a wedding ceremony or a graduation. Need fresh ideas to make baptism day special?

Invitations

Prepare printed invitations and e-mail invitations for baptismal services at your church, with blanks for adding the date, time, and name of the person being baptized. A new Christian most likely has an entire circle of friends and family who are still unbelievers. What a great time to reach out to them!

Stand Up, Friends

Make a baptismal service even more personal by asking friends and relatives of the new Christian to stand during the baptism. This request may be verbally stated during the baptism or printed in the program. An alternate suggestion: Before baptizing a new Christian, ask everyone present who has taught, shared a witness, or prayed for him or her to stand during the baptism. This could include acquaintances in Bible study, Sunday school teachers, discipleship leaders, choir leaders, friends, and relatives.

Read Their Testimony

Ask each baptismal candidate to write out a brief, clear personal testimony by finishing these three sentences.

"Before I received Jesus, my life was . . ."

"I came to realize I needed Jesus when . . ."

"I received Jesus into my life by . . ."

Laminate the printed testimony and read it from the baptistery. What an effective way to explain to guests how to know Jesus!

A Meaningful Memento

Create a computer-generated baptismal certificate, inserting a digital photo of the baptism. Add the new Christian's name, date of baptism, and church information. It may be signed by the pastor, a staff member, deacon, or baptismal committee chairperson. Present the certificate, along with the laminated testimony, as a reminder of this significant occasion.

Audiovisual

One slide of the preservice audiovisual could announce, "Jake Matheus will be baptized today!" During the baptism display the name of the baptismal candidate on the screen. Even better, show a live video of the baptism.

Take a Photo

If it's appropriate at your church, take a photograph from the side of the baptistry during the baptism.

A Confirming Question

"Jake, is it your testimony that you have asked Jesus Christ into your heart to be your Lord and Savior?" can be answered, "Yes, I have!"

All Together Now

If immediate family members are being baptized during the same service, an additional minister can join the pastor in the baptistry with them. Individually introduce, individually read testimonies, then baptize them at the same time.

Sunday Morning Baptism

If your church normally baptizes on Sunday evenings, consider celebrating it occasionally on Sunday morning. Most unsaved people attend during that service, and God can use those testimonies to touch lives.

A Traditional Song

After the last person was baptized, our church traditionally concluded each baptismal observance with the congregation joyously standing to sing the chorus "I Have Decided to Follow Jesus." Choose an appropriate chorus that fits your church's personality, and sing for joy to celebrate baptisms!

An Annual Montage

Create a cumulative montage with a video or still photo of each person baptized at your church that year. It should show celebration and joy and could be used in conjunction with a sermon about how God changes lives.

A Whole Worship Service

Did several youth receive Christ at youth camp? Was the evangelistic revival a life-changing event for many? If your church has many brand-new Christians at once, why not plan an entire worship service around those baptisms.

Celebrate New Birth

Need ideas to celebrate a friend or relative who is a new Christian awaiting baptism? See "New Christians" section for meaningful ideas.

Reception

Some churches prepare a celebration reception. In many churches in Germany, friends of the new Christian share encouraging words at an afternoon dessert fellowship.

The Time is Now

Yes, salvation is a personal decision. But if many attenders in your church are Christians who have never been baptized, plan an enormous baptism Sunday. Announce ahead of time that many will be baptized on that date, and ask them to make a reservation. Assign a church leader to each baptismal candidate to confirm his or her decision for Christ. The angels will rejoice!

Got Water?

If your church has no baptistry or is remodeling, find water! I've seen baptisms in a river, an apartment hot tub, a lake, a bathtub, a swimming pool, an ocean, a portable baptistery, and a horse trough! The Ethiopian eunuch said, "See, here is water. What hinders me from being baptized?" (Acts 8:36 NKJV).

Benevolence

*"The one who oppresses the poor insults their Maker,
but one who is kind to the needy honors Him."*

—Proverbs 14:31

Need fresh ideas to show his love to the poor in your church's community?

Project: Jesus Loves the Little Children

It's my favorite benevolence project. Create a huge "shopping" area at your church where you can distribute school supplies and kids' clothing and give free haircuts to underprivileged children. We used an outside pavilion; but a large classroom or fellowship hall would work well. Ask church members to bring backpacks, lunch boxes, and school supplies. Collect gently used shoes and clothing for kids and teens, along with new socks. Carefully organize clothing by size and supplies by grade supply lists. Obtain proper state approval so volunteer hairstylists can give haircuts for children. Treat every parent and child with dignity and Christian love. "Project: Jesus Loves the Little Children" will remind children of God's love for many months.

Build a Wall

Need to stock up supplies for your benevolence food pantry? Challenge youth to collect enough boxes of crackers or cans of vegetables to build a wall in the youth area of church.

The Great Giveaway

Organize a huge garage sale at your church but with a ministry twist: *Everything is free!* Church members contribute the furniture, bikes, clothes, trinkets, and treasures for the event. You might even have a used car! Add importance to the sale by using a large tent and playing recorded or live Christian music.

Organize the sale items attractively and set up a free lemonade and homemade cookies stand. All people who stop by are freely and joyfully given any and all items they desire, and absolutely no monetary donations are accepted. Of course, the giveaway refers to church members sharing the good news! Distribute Bibles or Jesus videos. Present each shopper with a witness tract and a printed invitation to church on Sunday.

Sock Tree

For a lovely and purposeful December benevolence project, invite church members to bring new socks of all colors and sizes to give to the less fortunate. As socks are collected, roll each pair into a ball and place it on a Christmas tree using an ornament wire. The sock tree will remind everyone to bring socks for the needy. Gloves work well for this project, too.

Christmas House

All year long stockpile toys that are donated to your church's benevolence ministry, then create a "Christmas store" for parents in need. Clean and repair the used toys, dolls, and bikes; then plan a free shopping day for the needy near Christmas. Allow parents to select a certain number of toys for each of their children. Serve punch, play Christmas music, and perform Christmas puppet shows to entertain kids while parents shop. All in Jesus' name!

Food Fight

Our church youth group's annual "food fight" replenished our benevolence food pantry each November. No, not *that* kind of food fight. Each grade challenged the others to see who could collect the most nonperishable food. During the three-hour event, they picked up bags of food from church members and friends. The team with the most pounds of food won the annual event, and the benevolence pantry was stocked for the holidays.

Soup Month

It may help replenish your church's food pantry to request specific staples. For example, post reminders around the church that September is Spam month or April is peanut butter month.

More than Food

All workers in a church benevolence ministry must be trained to share the gospel. At our church's food pantry, we took the client's food order first. While the order was being filled, the gospel was shared. Conversely, the gospel was shared as part of an exit interview at our free medical clinic.

Blogging

Can a blog enhance church ministry?

"Without guidance, people fall, but with many counselors there is deliverance."

—Proverbs 11:14

Even Paul sought to use every means to share Jesus. Would blogging benefit your church?

Testimonies

Invite church members to write out their Christian testimonies. Share one testimony on your blog each week with your congregation.

Staff meeting

You can create an ongoing staff meeting by blogging. In the busy lives of church staff, you can stay connected via the staff blog.

Photo Journal

A pastor or designated leader could create a photo journal blog, using words and photos to share blessings, events, and highlights of church life.

Communicate

Blogging can allow a minister to connect with church members throughout the week. He can teach, challenge, remind, and encourage members and readers. A blog poses an exceptional communication channel for reaching the youth in your church in a fun and innovative way.

Group Blog

Perhaps several church staff leaders could all post on a blog about your church lessening the burden on one person, increasing readership and adding variety.

Devotion

A pastor or church staff member can write a regular devotional thought and share it with your congregation by blogging. It could be tied to a current sermon theme or church goal.

Continued Thoughts

A pastor may sometimes have a thought after a sermon that would enhance what he just preached. He can encourage the congregation to check out his blog regularly for continued thoughts on the sermon topics.

Spiritual Journaling

Many bloggers use their blog for spiritual journaling. They simply type their thoughts and prayers as they spend time with God.

Prayer

You can keep your church members up-to-date with prayer concerns. Make policies to help with privacy issues.

Linked Blog

Place a link to the pastor or minister's blog from the church's Web site.

Limp Blog

If you blog, blog. Make a commitment to post a blog entry a minimum of once each week. Regular posts will keep readers returning. Failure to keep your blog updated will quickly deter your readers.

Blog Smog

Blogging could become burdensome, and might even negatively impact face-to-face effectiveness in ministry if you let it overtake your schedule. Commit a specific number of weekly hours to blogging. Most blogs encourage conversation and comments from readers; however, it is not necessary or desirable to respond to every comment posted.

Integrity

The element of open interaction gives blogging its appeal; however, the blogger should maintain integrity by removing inappropriate comments. Allow freedom of expression, but quickly remove comments that involve gossip, slander, inappropriate language, or heresy.

Building Dedication

*"Then the Israelites, including the priests, the Levites,
and the rest of the exiles, celebrated the dedication of
this house of God with joy."*

—Ezra 6:16

It's the culmination of months of hard work. Celebrate God's blessing of a new church building. Need fresh ideas?

First Sunday

Retail stores call it a "soft opening." The first Sunday you meet in your new church building will be a special day; however, the building dedication ceremony should be scheduled a few weeks later.

Building Dedication Ceremony Invitations

Print invitations for the ceremony, and mail them to as many people as possible. Send an invitation to every person who has attended your church during the past year. Invite local association and state convention representatives. Invite those who helped with constructing the building—construction workers, architects, contractors, volunteers, and the person who issued your building permit. Use reverse directories, Internet, or mail service to obtain addresses for all residences and commercial establishments near your church. Invite sister churches, political officials, fire department personnel, and the mail carrier. The more the merrier!

E-mail Invitations

Create an attractive e-mail invitation to the building dedication, and send it to every church member and prospective member. Request that they forward the invitation to everyone on their e-mail address list who might like to attend.

A Banner Invitation

It's worth the expense to purchase a large banner to place near the street, inviting the whole community to your building dedication. If you have a large "coming soon" sign already, simply install a diagonal overlay invitation on it.

The Ceremony

The building dedication ceremony will be brief and celebrative. The pastor may share Scripture, recognize the building committee and special guests, and lead the church in a prayer of thanksgiving to God. If the attendance is large, guests could be invited to encircle the building for a song or prayer. Everyone is then invited to take a self-guided tour of the new facility. Conclude with an informal reception and snacks.

Building Tour

A self-guided tour of the new building may be scheduled before or after the dedication ceremony. Station an enthusiastic church member in each room of the new building to explain the ministry purpose of that room and to point out unique features of the room. These guides could be church leaders, building committee members or volunteers. If the facility is large, give guests a map and place arrows in the hallways to direct guests through the facility. Display building plans and lots of photographs of the building project in progress.

Neighbors Only

Your church may additionally plan a "neighbors only" open house for the new building. Shortly after completion of the project, mail or deliver invitations to neighbors within a selected distance of your church, asking them to attend an informal "neighbors only" grand opening reception. Invite them to stop by to see the finished building project during a come-and-go half-hour reception. As they arrive, make them a name tag, complete with their address. Friendly church members may volunteer to assist church staff or deacons to greet and give guided tours, ending at a reception site where they receive refreshments and church members mingle and visit with guests. As they depart, give them a printed invitation to worship at your church on Sunday, along with a church brochure or DVD.

Flower Shower

A sister church or parent church may plan a separate event as a shower for your new church building. They should request a specific list of needs, and the shower gifts should directly benefit the new building. For example, if you've built a children's building, a toy shower would be appropriate. A new fellowship area might call for a kitchen shower or folding chair shower. A new church office suite? How about an office supply shower? They could plan a flower shower to help with bushes and landscape needs.

Note-Burning Ceremony

A church-wide celebration may be planned when a church mortgage has been paid in full. This can be a simple but significant ceremony, designed to praise God for his provisions. Consider doing the actual note-burning in an outdoor setting, if possible. I attended a note-burning ceremony where the sprinkler system went off when the paper burned! If you plan to actually ignite a piece of paper to represent the mortgage, use a large urn or an ornamental birdbath as a base.

Children's Area

"We must not hide them from their children, but must tell a future generation the praises of the LORD, His might, and the wonderful works He has performed."

—Psalm 78:4

There's nothing appealing about empty walls and stale paint. Freshen up your church's children's area!

"Hey, Lady, What Did You Learn at Church Today?"

As I walked through the children's area, a puppet in a tiny corner puppet theater asked me that question! The mini-puppet theater, a three-foot triangle, featured a clever puppeteer each Sunday between Sunday school and church.

On the Level

In children's hallways at church, mount signs and art at children's eye level.

Priceless Art

Ask children of all ages to submit their art in a collection box. Request that children use 8½-by-11-inch papers and write their name and phone number on the back. All art should have a Christian theme. Purchase several nice frames with quality matting or plastic box-type frames. Hang the frames in the children's hallway, and change the art regularly, displaying every piece of art that is submitted.

Corner Stage

It's a simple decorating idea. Build a simple small stage in an out-of-the-way corner of a common area. Make it just one step high, and paint brightly colored wood to look like curtains at the sides. A sign reads "Singing for Jesus." Add a fake microphone made of a tennis ball and paper towel roll. Children will love impromptu performing and praising God.

I Go to the Zaccheus Room!

Use Bible character names, Bible words, or art to identify individual classrooms in the children's area at church. Children will be excited, and parents can easily find their child's classroom.

Interactive Hallways

Make kids love their area at church! A huge paper roll could be mounted vertically on a focal wall, and new paper used each week to allow early arrivers to draw about that day's Bible lesson. An entire wall can be painted with chalkboard paint or covered with a giant whiteboard. Paint the words "God made everything" across the top and encourage children to praise him creatively with art. Some churches actually mount interactive objects on hallway walls, such as a knob on a small door to open, with a Scripture behind it. Or a mirror with a sign that says, "Who does God love?" An aquarium. A kid-sized stage in a corner. Get creative. Children should love to come to church.

Lions and Tigers and Trains

The children's area of church must be inviting and must enhance Bible teaching. If teachers are committed to making weekly visuals for teaching, simple solid-colored walls will suffice. A church may get creative with murals, colors, three-dimensional art, and interactive art to make a church's children's area enticing. Two rules: The theme must point to God, and the décor must be updated at least every five years. An animal theme could be tied to Noah's Ark or a "God Made the Animals" theme. A moving train could be mounted along the top of the hallway, with a transportation-themed mural of ways to praise Jesus (honk if you love Jesus, racing to Jesus, on track for Jesus, etc.).

Youth Decorators

Our church had an annual contest between youth Sunday school classes. Each class planned and painted their classroom walls, with just one rule: the theme must magnify God. The classrooms were absolutely fabulous!

Please Touch That Wall

To personalize a large wall in the youth or children's department, invite each person who attends to dip their palm in paint, put their handprint on the wall, and sign it. When guests visit, they add their handprint and name. It not only makes guests feel included; it makes a handsome wall.

Children's Involvement

"Let the little children come to Me."

—Mark 10:14

Teach children to love and serve a living God. Need fresh ideas?

The Right Kind of Heroes

When guest speakers or musicians visit your church, encourage children to get their autographs. My childhood pastor challenged kids at our church to collect autographs of revival speakers and missionaries in the flyleaf of our Bible. What a treasure I have in those!

Pastor's Pals Notebook

Pages in a Pastor's Pals notebook can have blanks for the date, sermon title, and Scripture text and room for children to draw something mentioned in the sermon each week.

Hi Luke! Glad You Came!

Give children simple responsibilities at church. For example, fifth graders could be assigned to collect the cups after each Lord's Supper service. A well-behaved child could serve alongside parents as a door greeter, concentrating on welcoming children.

I Commit $4.25 to the Building Fund

Allow children to make commitments to the church fund-raising efforts, whether for missions, building, or special projects.

If *They* Can Do It . . .

When our church was challenged to learn a difficult "Scripture of the year," my pastor-husband would give the Scripture text to one children's Sunday school department to learn ahead of time. On the first Sunday of the year, those children would quote the Scripture confidently. Even difficult passages were quickly learned by children. So if *they* can do it . . .

Sermon in a Sack

Pastor Larry Snyder, Victory Baptist in Clinton, Indiana, plans a two-minute mini-sermon for kids each Sunday during worship. Kids gather around him for a "Sermon in a Sack," an object lesson about the Bible. He uses a surprise item inside a brown paper bag to visually relate a Bible truth.

Only the Children On This Verse

Choose a familiar song during worship one Sunday, and invite "children only" to sing one verse. What a choir!

Kids in Charge

As a change of scenery, why not invite fifth-grade children to read the Scripture, lead a prayer, and pass the offering plate one Sunday?

Welcome to Big Church

It's an important day—the first day little children from the nursery area get to come to big church with their parents! Our church made a big deal of those children each year on promotion day, asking them to stand and receive their own Bible as a gift. This recognition also helped those seated nearby to encourage and help them feel welcome.

Train the Parents

Plan a class for parents of children promoting from the nursery to attend church services. Title it "Parents Guide for Bringing Little Kids to Big Church." Teach parents to choose carefully a location in the worship center that will interest the child, such as near the piano or drummer. Help them to plan ahead by going to the restroom before worship. My pediatrician once told me that a child without physical problems can easily wait an hour between bathroom breaks. Talk about how parents should involve their child in worship, singing, praying, participating in the offering, reading the Scripture from the Bible, and standing and sitting at the appropriate times. Help parents help children love church.

Mr. D. Josh. Mrs. Stinson. Hannah.

The children's choir could be interspersed among the adults in choir and worship team one Sunday during worship music. They'll love helping to lead worship, and children will make new adult Christian friends.

Just a Song

Your children's choir doesn't necessarily have to perform a concert when they sing in church. Just one short, well-prepared, heartfelt song makes a great impact on worship.

Parents Stand

After a children's choir sings in church, ask all of their parents to stand, then dismiss children to find their folks and sit with them during worship.

Children's Worship Bulletin

Our church printed a special Sunday worship bulletin for children. A church member prepared them, using puzzles and games related to the sermon topic for the day.

Best VBS Marketing

It's the best publicity plan for Vacation Bible School or children's events at church: Challenge children to invite their friends, neighbors, and classmates. Entrust them with flyers, tickets, and posters.

Church Workday

Instead of hiring child-care workers or sending children outside to play, include them in your church workdays. Make a list of jobs children can do and let them participate. For example, children may use oiled cloths to polish all the church pews.

My Prayer Hour

If your church has a prayer chapel or prayer chain, encourage children to participate with their parents or adult friends. God certainly hears their prayers!

Pinched Cheeks

They love well-behaved children at most nursing homes. Include your children in nursing home visits, homebound contacts, and benevolence deliveries when it's appropriate.

Christian Citizenship Sunday

"First of all, then, I urge that petitions, prayers, intercessions, and thanksgivings be made for everyone, for kings and all those who are in authority, so that we may lead a tranquil and quiet life in all godliness and dignity."

—1 Timothy 2:1–2

Patriotic Sundays can impact a lost world for Christ. Need fresh ideas?

Christian Citizenship Day

On the Sunday closest to July 4, plan a Christian citizenship emphasis. Post an outdoor sign and advertise in the local newspaper to invite the community to the patriotic-themed worship service. Decorate with flags and bunting. Prepare fabulous patriotic music. Most importantly, the entire worship service on patriotic days must point toward the God we serve and worship.

The Mayor's Coming to Church

Plan months ahead for Christian Citizenship Sunday. Mail invitations to community leaders. Invite state representatives, county officials, mayor, city council representatives, police and fire chiefs, school superintendent, school board members, etc. Reserve several pews for the honored guests and their families. Ask them to arrive early at the pastor's office for instructions and prayer. Introduce them during the worship service, and invite church members to stand to indicate that they will continue to pray for the community leaders.

That Church Prays for Me

As governmental leaders are recognized during Christian Citizenship Sunday, present them a memorial gift. A coffee mug, paperweight, pen, desk clock, or bookmark can be imprinted with the church's name and 1 Timothy 2:1–2.

Scouts or Royal Ambassadors

July 4 Sunday is a good time to ask a uniformed scout troop, Royal Ambassadors, or ROTC group to begin the service with a formal presentation of flags. Play a drum cadence as they enter.

Pray for Leaders

For the few Sundays preceding July 4, display a list of government leaders and invite church members to sign up to pray regularly for one of them. They can send occasional notes to remind that leader of their prayers.

Community Event

If your community has a big July 4 celebration, get involved. Your church choir or ensemble group could offer to set up a stage and perform patriotic music. Distribute helium balloons imprinted with "We love God and the freedom he gives!" Enter the best float in the parade. Rent a festival booth and distribute free water.

Invite Veterans on Veterans Day

Hang a banner outside and advertise in local newspapers to invite military personnel and veterans to attend worship on Veterans Day Sunday. Some may wear their uniforms. Invite church members to gather around them for prayer.

Silent Prayer

On Memorial Day or Veterans Day, allow a minute of silent prayer of thanksgiving to God for those who have given their lives for our country.

National Day of Prayer

Prepare a professionally painted exterior sign to invite the community to stop by the church to pray for our nation on the first Thursday of May each year. Open the church from 6:00 a.m. to 8:00 p.m. Quietly play recorded Christian music. At the entrance, provide a prayer list of national, state, and local leaders. A Day of Prayer guest book can be used again each year.

Christmas

"Today a Savior, who is Messiah the Lord,
was born for you . . ."

—Luke 2:11

It's time to shine, church! Need some fresh ideas?

Citywide Exhibit of Nativities

If some members of your church collect nativity scenes, display them beautifully at your church and advertise to invite the community for a one-day exhibit. Plan a preview exhibit on Sunday before the event so church members can enthusiastically spread the word and bring guests. Create ambiance with recorded or live Christmas music, and offer hot punch and cookies for guests. Place cards at each nativity scene can give interesting details. A greeter can present each guest with a printed brochure to explain the life-changing significance of the nativity and invite them to upcoming Christmas events.

Christmas Port-a-Party

Invite prospective members to this fun party. Decorate a bus or van exterior with battery-operated Christmas lights and gaudy decorations. A driver dressed as Santa chauffeurs guests to four class member's homes for stand-up salad, soup, entrée, and dessert courses. En route to the homes, additional stops are planned for caroling to a homebound member, a group photo at a beautiful site, and gift exchange at your town's Christmas tree. Plan a scenic Christmas light route, and serve cocoa from thermoses on the ride home. Present copies of the group photo as a memento.

Live Sheep

Nothing stops traffic like live animals. Give your community a very special gift—a live nativity scene. Build a simple stable on your church lawn. Add bright spotlights, amplified Christmas music, and some staked live stable animals. Make two complete sets of one-size-sits-all costumes and props, and schedule church members in half-hour shifts to portray nativity characters—angels, shepherds, kings, Mary and Joseph. Use a life-like doll for the baby, Jesus. Our church's live nativity scene was done on the first weekend of December, and it was a great community witness as well as lots of fun for participants. Shifts for the live nativity were staffed by adults, youth, and children. Advertise well. Give onlookers hot cocoa and a card explaining the true meaning of Christmas. Invite each guest to worship on Sunday.

Drive-Thru Nativity

If your church has a large parking lot or circular drive, prepare several wooden backdrops depicting each scene of the nativity story. Costumed characters and animals pose to reenact the scenes. Prepare a CD with a well-worded description of Jesus' birth, complete with background music. Beeps indicate when the car should progress to the next scene, and the audio can include an invitation to Sunday worship. As cars enter the church parking lot, present each person with a cup of hot chocolate and the CD and ask them to listen as they drive through the scenes.

Drive-Thru Christmas Carols

Use the same idea above, but create backdrops to illustrate several Christmas carols that tell the Christ story. Live, costumed church members pose as nativity characters. Woodworkers and artists used plywood to create huge, hinged "Christmas cards" which were spectacular to view and simple to store.

Christmas Luncheon

My favorite Christmas outreach event is a ladies' Christmas luncheon. Use church members' nativity scenes for fabulous centerpieces. The program consists of beautiful Christmas music and an inspirational Christian speaker. Sell tickets so members can present them as gifts to friends.

Nativi-Tea

Challenge church members to invite neighbors to their home for a tea or neighborhood open house. Using a nativity scene, they can explain why Christmas means so much to them and invite neighbors to attend Christmas services with them. Your church could design a special brochure for all members to use at their teas, telling the real story of Christmas and inviting neighbors to Christmas services.

Christmas Parade

No Christmas parade in your town? Plan your own church's nativity parade and invite the community. Plan carefully and involve the entire church to present visually each part of the nativity story. If it isn't possible to use city streets, stage the parade in your church parking lot. Various Bible classes or groups in the church volunteer to prepare fabulous floats, and each one represents a part of the Christmas story. Students could form a marching band or strolling singers. All the children could dress as shepherds riding bicycles or skating angels. The pastor and his wife act as the "grand marshals." If the parade is in your church parking lot, floats could be pulled by riding lawn mowers. Give each parade onlooker a printed invitation to Sunday worship and other Christmas events at your church.

Nativity Music

Music for one December worship service could feature a simple stable onstage, with a costumed Mary, Joseph, and baby Jesus. As the congregation sings appropriate Christmas carols, costumed angels, then shepherds, and then kings approach the stable to worship the Child as each new song begins. Lastly, an assortment of modern-day worshippers joins them to worship Jesus as you sing "Oh, Come All Ye Faithful."

Nativi-Tree

A children's Sunday school class can make ornaments for a Christmas tree displayed in a foyer. They can make stars, angels, and the whole nativity to illustrate the Christmas story.

A Nativity-a-Day

For a ministry project, purchase a twelve-piece nativity scene and do this version of the Twelve Days of Christmas for a homebound member or person who will be alone for the first time this Christmas. Deliver one piece of the nativity scene daily for twelve days, ending with baby Jesus on Christmas day. If this is a church or class project, a different member could deliver each day. A friend of mine did this with secret deliveries, leaving daily notes and gift-wrapped nativity pieces on the front porch. At a scheduled time, she and her family delivered the baby on Christmas day.

Family Nativity Party

At a Christmas party for families in your church, make beautiful nativity scenes as a craft project. Whether it's ceramic, painted wood, or even Popsicle sticks and peanuts, it will be a treasure for years to come.

Handcrafted Ornaments

Begin in January to plan a unique Christmas tree for the church foyer. A designer chooses a color scheme and gives patterns or ideas to various members to make one fabulous ornament before next November. The theme could be names for Christ, symbols of Christ, or nativity characters. The ornaments could be embroidered, sequined, painted fabric or another medium.

Skating Shepherds

Create a fabulous nativity float for your town's holiday parade. Ask teens or older children from your church to dress as shepherds or angels and skate or walk alongside the float to distribute brochures you've created to explain the eternal meaning of Christmas.

Nativity Children's Sermon

One Christmas our pastor asked children to sit on the steps near the pulpit as he preached the Christmas story. He had given each child a piece from a nativity scene, secretly keeping the baby Jesus figurine in his pocket. As he shared the Christmas story, the children reverently brought the appropriate pieces to place in the stable. He pretended to end the story without mentioning the baby, Jesus. As he paused, one small boy stood up unprompted, put his hands on his hips and shouted, "Wait! You can't have Christmas without the baby Jesus!" What a perfect illustration!

Advent

Create excitement and anticipation by celebrating Advent the four Sundays before Christmas. The candle lighting is simple to plan, takes only a couple of minutes during worship, and is meaningful to all. Ask an artistic member to make an Advent wreath, and then invite a different family to light the candle and present the prayer each week. Visit your Christian bookstore to select a script that fits your church.

A Christmas Program

If your church presents a special Christmas musical or drama, design it for those outside the church. Church members can distribute free "tickets" for invitations. Treat nonmembers who attend as special guests, not as outsiders.

A Walk through Bethlehem

Consider recreating the city of Bethlehem as an outreach event for your community. Many churches across our country use a variety of methods, so research some of them for success tips. Basically, a working first-century town is created with a reenactment of the Christmas story, using story-teller guides who take small groups on a tour. Preparation will involve draftsmen, carpenters, seamstresses, and construction workers. Dozens of church members will play the parts of city dwellers and tour guides. Live animals add authenticity. A costumed pastor or church leader can present the last scene, a cross and the empty tomb, with an evangelistic witness. Be prepared: you may have hundreds or even thousands of attenders! Lots of work? Yes. Worth the effort? Definitely.

Christmas Cookies for Cops

As a church-wide or class project, prepare and deliver Christmas goodies to public servants in your town—a local fire department, police station, mayor's office, school staff, etc. Include a note of sincere appreciation and an invitation to special Christmas services.

Free Childcare

Plan a special party night for children, and allow parents to go shopping one weekday during December. Ask church members to spread the word to unchurched friends and neighbors about the free shopping time. Require reservations for proper planning. When parents hear how much their child loved it, they'll want to come back on Sunday!

Church Decorations

We decorate the inside of our churches beautifully, but the outside world only sees the exterior! Next year, why not consider investing in a gorgeous lighted nativity scene, outdoor lighting, beautiful wreaths for your doors, or a big star mounted above your church.

Great Wall of Boxes

If your church collects shoebox gifts for seamen, local ministries, or Operation Christmas Child, challenge the church to build a whole "wall of boxes." Begin building the wall in an appropriate area, and show photos in church of how the wall is progressing.

A Gift-Wrapped Ministry

Set up a free gift-wrap table at a local mall, purchase bulk rolls of paper, then joyfully wrap gifts for shoppers. Distribute a printed invitation to church Christmas events.

Christmas Caroling

Spice up your caroling
this Christmas.
You've got something
to sing about!

*"Sing to Him; sing praise to Him;
tell about all His wonderful works!"*

—1 Chronicles 16:9

What a great time to tell the world about Jesus! Everyone loves carolers. Need fresh ideas?

Frozen Carolers

It feels more like Christmas if carolers wear coats, scarves, and muffs. Even in warm weather, ask your Christmas caroling participants to dress like they're cold. You might even enjoy tossing a little fake snow!

Decorate Your Chariot

Whether your Christmas carolers are traveling by bus, van, or cars, embellish the vehicles with signs, gaudy decorations, and battery-powered lights. The neighborhood will notice.

Can You Kazoo?

Bring kazoos for all your Christmas carolers, and play in harmony for an interlude or a verse. You'll be amazed at how great it sounds.

Love Note

Ask all the carolers to sign a Christmas card to leave at each residence where you'll carol.

Dazzling

For a brilliant performance, carolers can hold strings of battery-powered Christmas lights.

Jingle Bells

Christmas carolers can use tiny jingle bells for extra pizzazz. Or for a snazzy intro, Christmas carolers can play the first two bars of "Joy to the World" on handbells. No talent is required, just an extra minute of rehearsal.

Cup of Christmas Cocoa

Your Christmas caroling group can bring a thermos of cocoa, plastic cups, and canned whipping cream, serving a warm drink to each spectator as they carol. Ladies' daytime carolers could purchase a Christmas teacup and saucer as a gift and serve hot tea as they carol.

Party with Purpose

Begin the church choir's Christmas party with a caroling blitz. Divide into quartets and carol for homebound or nursing home residents, then meet back together for the party.

Homemade Ornament

Before caroling, make Christmas ornaments as gifts to present when you go caroling. Fill glass balls with sparkles, decorate them to honor Jesus' birthday, and add the year and church name.

Nursing Home Parade

Costume your children's group as kings, shepherds, angels, animals, Mary and Joseph. Use a doll to represent baby Jesus. With permission from the retirement center's director, stage a Christmas caroling parade through the hallways, then pose as a nativity for caroling in the common area.

Add an Instrument

Add just one musical instrument to your Christmas caroling group—a flute, d'jembe, guitar, trumpet, accordion. Almost any instrument will work. Tell the instrumentalists ahead of time what carols you'll sing.

Fashion Statement

Add a little interest to your group's appearance. Everyone could wear the same colors. They could all wear hats. They could all wear house slippers or ties or choir robes. Everyone loves carolers dressed in Victorian clothing.

It's a Gift

Remove the top and bottom of boxes, cut armholes on sides, and gift-wrap them. The kids' choir can wear them for caroling in the neighborhood. For the final touch, place bows on their heads. The children can prepare handmade notes that declare, "The greatest gift is Jesus!" Note: you'll need an extra pickup truck to transport the boxes if you carol away from the church neighborhood.

Short and Sweet

The best Christmas carolers leave the listeners wanting more. Simply sing the first verse of three familiar carols, then "We Wish You a Merry Christmas" as the group waves good-bye.

You're Caroling Where?

Choose unexpected places to carol—the fire station, the homeless, your apartment balcony, a bus stop. Where better than a shopping mall to share Jesus at Christmas? Hospitals, office buildings, and malls may enthusiastically schedule groups to carol in their atrium. Call early in November for scheduling, and share the songs of Christmas with your community. With permission from the mall, display an attractive poster on an easel inviting listeners to hear more beautiful music at your church's worship services on Sunday.

Reverse Caroling

Teens love this silly idea. They show up at a youth worker's or church family's home, pretending to be carolers. When the family opens the door, they give them songbooks for reverse Christmas caroling. That means the visited people sing! "First song is 'Joy to the World!' 1, 2, 3, Go!"

Singing on the Street

Display a big sign on the church lawn: "Outdoor Carolers Nightly, 7–8 p.m." Place a spotlight for the carolers in a visible area, roping a side area for spectators. Carefully schedule twenty-minute shifts for caroling groups, staffed by your church choirs, ensembles, senior saints, finance committee, Bible class, preschoolers, women's group, teens, etc. Designate a few shifts "Everybody sings!" with one person in charge and all church members invited to stop by and sing during that shift. Of course, the leader would recruit a few people ahead of time. You'll be amazed at what fun your church softball team or deacons will have, joyfully singing about Jesus' birth for everyone who drives past the church.

Christmas Eve Service

"God's love was revealed among us in this way: God sent His One and Only Son into the world so that we might live through Him."

—1 John 4:9

A Christmas Eve service is a meaningful tradition for church members and a fabulous community outreach opportunity for your church.

Community Invitation

Invite the entire community. Advertise your church's Christmas Eve services in the local paper and on outdoor signs or banners at your church. You'll be surprised at how many unchurched people may venture in!

Best Music of the Year

Finalize Christmas Eve music plans before Thanksgiving, and invite your church's best soloists or ensembles. Music for multiple services may be vary but top quality is a essential. A live instrumental prelude would welcome guests beautifully.

Christmas Communion

Your church may enjoy concluding the service with a reverent observance of the Lord's Supper.

He Is the Light

Display five candles at the front of the worship center. As the pastor reads the Christmas story, he lights a candle to represent Mary, Joseph, shepherds, kings, and Jesus. As the pastor ends the story, he explains that each of the characters in the story eventually died, and he blows out each candle. The only remaining light in the room is the candle representing Jesus as he shares how Jesus died and rose again and lives today. (Alternate: use a relighting candle for the Jesus candle.)

Carry the Light

Give each person a candle as they arrive. At the conclusion of the service, challenge each person to carry the light of Jesus as they go out. Dim the lights as the pastor lights his candle from the Christ candle of the Advent wreath or from the Jesus candle (above). He then lights the candle of deacons or staff members, who light others, until the entire room is filled with candlelight.

Candlelight

A Christmas candlelight service needs lots of candles. Invite one family in your church to be responsible for preparing and lighting candles for each service. Dim the overhead lights and enjoy the warm atmosphere they create.

Greeters

Greeters could be entire families, several single adults, or staff families. Recruit them during November, inviting them to dress in their Christmas best, arrive half an hour early, and joyfully greet every guest.

Multiple Services

By offering two or more Christmas Eve services, your attendance will be greatly enhanced. Services can be identical or totally different. Our church planned three forty-five minute services at 4:00, 6:00, and 11:00 p.m.

Christmas Offering

Give attenders an opportunity to contribute to the budget or missions offering.

It's Tradition

By planning your church's Christmas Eve services every year, it will become a tradition for families in your church and community. It may be a dress-up affair, with everyone sporting their Christmas best, or it may be come-as-you-are casual. Either way it will create lasting Christmas memories.

Church Anniversary

Celebrating a round-
number church
anniversary? Do it
well!

*"In the future, when your children ask you, 'What do
these stones mean to you?' you should tell them . . ."*

—Joshua 4:6–7

If your church is going to celebrate a big anniversary, do it "as unto the Lord"!
Need fresh ideas?

The Biggest Secret
The biggest secret for planning a successful church anniversary or reunion
celebration is "plan ahead!" Schedule the date at least a year in advance and
send a "save this date" note to every former staff member or church member.

Detective
Designate a "detective" or detective team to locate every former staff member
and church member. Begin at least a year ahead to make a complete list. In
your church newsletter or bulletin, print a request for assistance with finding
current addresses or e-mail addresses.

Time Line
Create a time line, marking significant events in your church's history. Display
it down a central hallway of the church.

Salvations Spotlight

To focus attention on people who were saved over the years, use your church records to list every person baptized, in chronological order. That's what it's all about!

Drama Story

At their fiftieth church anniversary, First Baptist Evansville, Indiana, reenacted the story of the church's early history in a brief but powerful, drama. A member of the church wrote and produced it, using church members as actors. An animated narrator described an action-packed history while actors mimed the story.

History Book

Consider commissioning an author to write the church history. Invite church members and guests to reserve a book by purchasing it online. Release the publication at the anniversary celebration.

Church Cookbook

Publish a cookbook in conjunction with the anniversary. As former members' addresses are discovered, invite them to submit a favorite recipe, along with their favorite Scripture.

The Membership List

Use church records to make a huge list of every person who ever joined the church, in order of date. You could print it twice, showing names both in alphabetical order and by date they joined. Place the long list in an entry area, and encourage quests to initial by their name as they arrive.

Fifty years/Fifty Hours of Prayer

On the weekend of the celebration, plan a fifty-hour prayer event. Make the number of hours match the number of years you're celebrating. Create a large chart listing each hour time slot, and begin weeks ahead to allow members to commit to come to the church and pray for one specific hour. Create a worshipful atmosphere in a designated prayer area, using candles and a suggested prayer guide. Or create a unique prayer labyrinth and open the prayer room for all members to stop by for prayer, with designated leaders each hour. Thank God for past blessings and pray for the future of the church.

Anniversary Gift

Order a unique personalized gift for attendees at your church anniversary. It could be a paperweight, T-shirt, magnet, coin, notebook, bookmark, ornament, etc. Distribute the gift to each person who attends.

Video Story

Prepare a several-minute professional video story of the church's history to use as part of the day's program. Enhance its presentation by asking men, costumed for the appropriate time era, to dress as different pastors from history. Attempt to select men with similar physical characteristics of that pastor, i.e. tall, thin, balding, etc. While the video tells the story of that pastor's time period, the gentleman walks across the stage holding a sign, "Pastor Jim Jones, 1930–1945." The current pastor can portray himself.

Add a Steeple

Invite those who attend the anniversary celebration to participate in an offering for a specific big-dollar item that's needed by the church. It could be a stained-glass window, a prayer chapel, a steeple, an adjacent acre of land.

Eighty Years of Christian Music

For a fun outdoor afternoon picnic concert, plan a chronological concert for the number of years your church has been in existence. For example, if your church is celebrating its eightieth anniversary, begin the concert with "old-time religion" tunes and end with the top current Christian song.

Pictures, Pictures, and More Pictures

You can't have too many pictures. Ask a creative scrapbooker to prepare a history book of photographs. Create a looping audiovisual of hundreds of photos, and play it all day long on televisions around the building, at receptions, preservice and postservice. Make photo displays of pastors, buildings, youth events, etc. If you have full-length photographs of every pastor, consider enlarging them to life-size cardboard statues, and post dates on them.

Stand Up

During part of the anniversary celebration day, recognize the following people:
- Former pastors
- Current pastors
- Former staff members

- Current staff members
- Charter members
- Those baptized in the church
- Former deacons
- Current deacons
- Former Sunday school teachers
- Current Sunday school teachers
- Former and current choir members, orchestra members, age-group graded choir leaders, etc.
- Current church members
- People who initiated significant ministries of the church, i.e. library, benevolence ministry, day care
- Famous firsts, i.e. first youth minister, first pastor, first deacon ordained, first person baptized

The Way It Was

Instead of a luncheon speaker, consider asking five articulate members to share about the way it was at your church during a specific decade.

Online Dinner Reservations

Ask attenders to RSVP by mail or online. It is appropriate to ask attenders to purchase tickets for the luncheon, and many out-of-towners will appreciate the ability to make reservations online. If orders will be placed for T-shirts, cookbooks, or history books, allow payment and reservations for those online.

Registration

Several attractive registration tables should be staffed by friendly church members, preferably newer members who won't be too distracted when former members arrive. Give each attender a complete listing of anniversary events. When we attended the twenty-fifth anniversary of University Baptist, San Antonio, a church we helped plant, we were excited to receive a special emblem on our name tags as charter members and former pastor.

The Rule for Name Tags

When providing name tags for any event, here's the primary rule: the name must be readable from six feet away. That means preprinted name tags must use a huge font. It means that large-tipped black markers must be provided for name tags where attenders write their own name. Now, *that* name tag is worthwhile.

Sixty Years of Fashion

Add fun by inviting participants to dress in costume from any of the decades you're celebrating, including today's time period (for those who don't care to wear costumes). Award prizes for the best costumes before the day is over.

Don't Forget

For those attending the church anniversary, the greatest delight will be time spent with Christian friends. The schedule should include plenty of opportunities for casual fellowship.

Church Exterior

The exterior of your church shouts at those passing by! What does it say?

"You are the light of the world. A city situated on a hill cannot be hidden."

—Matthew 5:14

For all those people in your town who haven't come inside your church building yet, the church exterior is a strong witness. Need some fresh ideas?

Crooked Church Sign

Does your church sign entice those passing by to come in? Is your church sign fresh, clean, first-class, and inviting? Are the church phone number, Web site, and worship time stated? Is the sign clearly visible from the main street? A quality church sign is an excellent, necessary investment for any church.

Light Up

Consider this question: What is the best exterior feature of your church? Is it a steeple, a stained glass, an architectural element, a fabulous tree? Draw attention to that feature using spotlights or up-lights. Put stained-glass or unique windows on timers so they're visible in the evenings. Does landscape need spotlights? Is the church sign illuminated?

Kids Welcome Here

Does your church's exterior scream, "We love families"? Would it be feasible to designate preschool parking near the preschool entrance? Is your church playground the cleanest and most enticing in town? A new paint available at hardware stores does miracles for old metal or plastic playground equipment.

Something's Happening Here

Many unchurched people drive past your church regularly. Turn their head! Combat sameness with changeable signs, event banners, flags, outdoor activities, and tasteful displays. Draw attention for an event by renting a searchlight, flocking the lawn with flamingos, or staging human signboards. Our historic church rented a thirty-foot gorilla balloon to advertise a jungle-themed Vacation Bible School. Attendance soared!

That Back Wall

If a rear exterior wall is visible but windowless, would a Christian mural be attractive?

Yes, It's a Church

Does something on the exterior of your church building point toward the One you worship? A cross? A steeple? Bushes trimmed to spell *faith*? Consider a way you can convey to those passing by that your building is a house of God.

Image Maker Acre

If your church property is large, consider creating a walking trail interspersed with Scriptures on signs. Encourage your community to use it.

Peeling Paint or Perky Pansies

Walk outside and look critically at your church building as a passerby would see it. Old-timers and newcomers to your community have an opinion of your church derived from what they see on the outside. Does the building enhance the neighborhood? Is it clean, painted, and updated? Is the lawn manicured meticulously and carefully landscaped? Are sidewalks swept and fresh flowers planted during summer months?

Flyby Witness

If your church is located beneath an airline flight pattern, consider writing "God loves you" in huge letters on a flat roof or planting trees or bushes to spell *God* from above.

Plant a Tree

If landscape around your church building is lacking, have a landscape architect or landscape afficionado draw up a master plan, then get started. This is one of the least expensive but most impressive ways to beautify your church exterior.

Secret Church

Can guests easily find your church? Do you need additional directional signs? Use a professional sign company to help guests find your church.

Church Facilities

"Is it a time for you yourselves to live in your paneled houses, while this house lies in ruins?"

—Haggai 1:4

How much does your church love God? For a clue to the answer, take a look at the church facilities.

The Thirty-Second Rule

Walk into each entry area of your church and consider how it would look to a first-time guest. Observations made during the first thirty seconds are difficult to change later. Is it perfectly clean? Free of clutter? Is it well lit? Is it freshly painted and nicely decorated? Does it reflect your love of God?

Welcome to ABC Baptist

Personalized entry rugs may be ordered with the church logo or motto.

Fellowship Wall

To encourage fellowship, a church could display a large city map with a colored pin marking where every member lives.

Name Tags Wall

Many churches ask everyone to wear name tags to enhance fellowship. I've been to several churches with an attractive cabinet at the main entry that contains professional-looking plastic name tags for every member of the church. Members take their name tag as they enter and redeposit it as they leave. When new members join the church, they are presented their name tag at the next service. This method also helps to identify guests—those people without permanent name tags!

Funeral and Wedding Guests

When guests enter your building for a reception, funeral, or wedding, or even to work on the plumbing, what do they learn about your church and God by walking through the building? Is current church information easily available? Does the wall décor tell more about wealthy donors or church history than about a relevant and living God? Are bulletin boards current and enticing? Are hallways used for storage? Consider placing brochures about your church beliefs, i.e. Baptist Faith and Message, in a visible area. Photos, promotional posters, statistics, missions emphases—all these things can impact strangers who walk through your church building.

God's Artwork

Fresh flowers from a florist or a member's garden can add a classy touch to common areas of the church. A member of our church brought fresh flowers from her garden for various common areas of our church every Sunday. Can you guess what comment we heard most from guests?

Holy Walls

Scripture makes a lovely wall décor. You can order gorgeous framed Scriptures and choose a fitting verse for different areas of the church. Paintings can point people to Christ if an engraved metal plate with an appropriate Scripture is mounted on it.

Green Is Good

It's amazing how plants can enhance your church décor. Carefully select live or quality artificial plants, using attractive pots and strategic placement. Invite a church member with a green thumb to care for live plants regularly. Keep plant leaves clean and shined.

Art with Heart

Once each year, ask artistic church members to submit art with a Christian theme for one-year display at the church. Some churches use members' art for bulletins, programs, or church newsletters.

It's a Sign

If you want guests to feel welcome, it is essential that your church has excellent directional signs throughout. Walk in at every entrance, pretending to be a guest. Is there a directional sign that points you toward the worship center, the child-care area, the restrooms? Can a guest easily find your welcome center, library, offices? Are room numbers logically assigned and simple to locate?

No Extra Charge

A well-planned color scheme, carried throughout the church building, will greatly enhance the appearance of your church. It costs no more money to paint your walls "salmon alabaster" than to paint them white, but the ambiance is affected in a major way. Before you paint a white wall, ask someone with decorating sense to help choose a contemporary color, even if it's a neutral shade. When our church built an educational building, a choice of five colors was given to each Bible class for the accent wall in their classroom.

Not Negative

Avoid negative signs in your church facility. For example, instead of a "No Talking!" sign, print "Shhh! Worship in progress." Instead of "No Parking!" print, "Reserved for our handicapped friends." Instead of "No running," print, "Please walk."

Granny Smith Bought This Pew

If it is necessary to eternally honor those who donated the chandelier or furniture, do it discretely. The focal point at church should be God Almighty, not old man Johnson. He'll receive his accolades in heaven!

Older than Dirt

Even grocery stores change their carpet, update color schemes, and rearrange shelving every five years to keep it attractive for their customers. You'd never find ancient plastic flowers, dollar-store art, secondhand furniture or gold shag carpet there. God's house is much more important than Kroger.

Avoid "Old"

Many churches have an "old" fellowship hall or an "old" auditorium. When you construct a new fellowship hall, the "old" fellowship hall should receive a new name, such as "the parlor" or "room 12". If you refer to it as the "old" fellowship hall, you exclude and confuse newcomers.

Church Office

"But everything must be done decently and in order."

—1 Corinthians 14:40

Yes, it's an office. But it's also a ministry mobilization center. Need fresh ideas?

Savvy Screensavers

Your church office computers can help point guests to Christ. Bless people who walk through the office by using Scripture, church logo, photos of recent church events or church members, or church motto on computer screensavers.

Phone-Tree Manners

It's a great invention! A phone-tree is an inexpensive, small machine that can be programmed to call your church members' phones to leave a recorded message. For example, it can dial specific committee members for a meeting notice or dial the entire church to remind them about daylight savings time change. Snow cancellation? Use the phone tree. Some churches send a weekly message to members with current announcements. It's important, however, to word your message carefully and to limit the number of recorded calls your members receive.

De-clutter

Stand back and view your church office as a first-time visitor would see it. Carefully assure that its appearance honors your God. Does your church office area reflect your love for Christ? De-clutter entryways, floors, desktops, and closets. Apply fresh paint every few years. Rearrange occasionally. Old Sunday school literature probably doesn't need to be kept for decades. The donkey from last year's Christmas program belongs in storage. One small family photo looks better on a receptionist's desk than a personal gallery. A framed Scripture or Christian art is more appropriate than some types of wall hangings. You'll be amazed at how the entire atmosphere changes.

The $39 Solution

It's not a new invention, but more than half of churches in America aren't using an answering machine for after-hour calls. If the telephone at your church rings on Saturday morning or Tuesday evening, will the caller be able to discover Sunday worship times? Install one today.

It Doesn't Answer Unless

Turn your church answering machine on twenty-four hours per day, seven days per week. Disable call blocking. Set it to answer after one or two rings. In the recording, be sure to state the church name, address, worship time, and Web address.

My Church's Personality

The church answering machine message should reflect the personality of your church. The message can include directions, church motto, Scripture, or schedule. Some church recordings mention the week's special church events, an offer of prayer or transportation, or an enthusiastic welcome for guests to come to worship on Sunday.

A Good Habit

Consistently print the church Web site address on everything that leaves the church office—brochures, bulletins, newsletters, banners, printed pencils, etc.

Clergy Appreciation Day

*"Give recognition to those who labor among you and
lead you in the Lord."*

—1 Thessalonians 5:12–13

Each October many churches designate a day to show appreciation to their
pastor and church ministerial staff members. Need fresh ideas?

One Fishing Lure

Determine one small item your pastor enjoys, such as M&Ms, fishing lures,
popcorn, or golf balls. Ask each church member, including children, to bring
one of that item on pastor appreciation Sunday. For example, each person will
bring one bag, any size, of peanut M&Ms. Bring extras for guests and forgetful
members. As your church thanks God for your pastor, each member can walk
to the front and place their token of love in a large basket.

The Church Building and the Church

Present your pastor with a beautifully framed photo or painting of the church
building. Use an extra wide matting and ask all church members to sign the
mat before adding glass.

E-Pounding

Distribute your minister's e-mail address to all church or class members,
asking each one to send an e-mail note, describing something specific they
appreciate about their pastor. E-mails should be sent one specific day or week,
creating an e-pounding of blessings!

Text-Pounding

Use the same basic idea, but ask each member to send a text-message to the pastor or staff member.

Puzzle Gift

Order a jigsaw puzzle with a photo of your church family or church building. Internet puzzle companies make one-hundred or one-thousand piece puzzles from a photo.

Love Our Pastor

Take out a full-page ad in your local newspaper, featuring a photo of your pastor with church members' signatures around it. Include a declaration of your church's love and appreciation for your pastor.

Lotsa Notes

Give each church member a stamped envelope that is pre-addressed to your minister's home. Ask them to send a personal note of appreciation.

Make It a Month

As a church, deacon body, ladies group, choir, or youth group, make October a true *month* of appreciation for your pastor. Ask individual volunteers from the group to write their name on one day of an October calendar. On the assigned day, that person expresses appreciation to the pastor in a unique way. Each day will be different. The pastor might receive a letter or gift. It could be a meal, a shoeshine, or a "thank you" balloon bouquet. After a whole month of pleasant surprises, won't your pastor feel appreciated? And won't God be honored by your acts of love for his servant?

While You Were Out

Hanover Baptist in Indiana surprised their pastor with a gorgeous new home office. With his wife's input, of course, they worked with a decorator and volunteers to turn a spare room into a home office while the pastor was out of town. They did paint, wallpaper, window coverings, shelves, desk, chair, computer, and decorator items.

Gift of Prayer

Give your pastor the gift of prayer. Create a chart, and allow members to choose a specific time that they will commit to pray weekly for the pastor this next year. They do not need to come to a specific place, just pray on their way to work or pray each Tuesday at 2:00 p.m. The project could be done by a deacon group, choir, class, or the entire church. Present the prayer promise chart to the pastor as a gift. Then remember to pray!

A Class Idea

All the Sunday school classes of the church could pool their resources to purchase a full set of Bible commentaries. Every individual class could sign inside one of the books, then present it as a gift from their class.

Gift from Deacons

Each deacon purchases a gift certificate to a restaurant, car wash, coffee shop, or bookstore. He writes a personal note on the back, and all coupons are placed inside a card for the pastor.

Gift from Kids

Wouldn't it be fun for every child at church to create a signed bookmark for their pastor or children's pastor, using cardstock paper and crayons or markers? Laminate the bookmarks, and then call all the children forward at the end of worship to put their bookmarks in a basket for the pastor.

Gift from Youth

Create huge poster board hearts and a giant love note for everyone to read. Place them on stakes in your pastor's front yard during pastor appreciation day. You could add balloons but not toilet paper.

More Ideas for a Gift from the Church

Restaurant certificates, magazine subscription, tires, Bible software, a trip, a book, theater or sports tickets, flowers for his wife, babysitting coupons, a new car, a grandfather clock, a suit for the pastor and a dress for his wife, a new car, a new desk, home landscaping.

Say It

Write your minister an encouraging note the first day of every month this year. Tell him how last Sunday's sermon impacted your week. Take him to lunch and tell him how much you appreciate him as your pastor.

May I Borrow Your Car?

As a special surprise during Minister Appreciation Week, borrow your pastor's car and have it detailed, oiled and lubed, washed, and gassed.

Brag about Him

Brag about your pastor every chance you get and not just at church. Write a letter to the editor of a local newspaper during Minister Appreciation Month to compliment your minister.

"Pastor"

Show respect by calling him "pastor."

Personalized T

During Minister Appreciation Week, present him a "Best Pastor in Madison" T-shirt, substituting your town's name.

Take Care

During Minister Appreciation Week, anonymously mow and edge your pastor's lawn. Provide a generous book allowance for him in your church budget. Be sure that he's paid an appropriate salary. When he has houseguests coming, deliver a great casserole. Exempt clergy from bringing dishes to pitch-in dinners.

Love His Family

Do something special for your pastor's wife. Help pay for his teens to attend the church's youth retreat. Babysit his kids for free during a wedding or funeral. Include his family in your holiday celebration. Help his children apply for college scholarships. Deliver a Thanksgiving turkey to his house.

Quit Complaining

Quit complaining. Quit complaining. Quit complaining. Quit complaining.

College Student Encouragements

"Therefore encourage one another and build each other up . . ."

—1 Thessalonians 5:11

Whether they're away at university or attending one near your church, college students need your church's care. Want some fresh ideas?

Head Start

During summer before a freshman goes to college, your church's youth minister or youth leader can submit names and contact information to the leader of that school's campus ministry. For example, many Baptist collegiate ministers (see www.student.org) will write them, put welcome signs on their dorm room door, pray for them, and contact them personally. These important leaders will also encourage the students to become actively involved in a local church in their new location.

Adopt a Student

If your church is located near a university, invite families in your church to "adopt" a student. Families invite their adopted student for occasional meals, help them learn the community, and offer to let them do laundry at their house. They may include the student in holiday celebrations if they are in town. They can help to disciple and encourage the student. Assign adoptions in August, with a request that families get together with their student at least monthly.

Welcome Day

Plan a special welcome service for college students on a Sunday early in the fall semester. Serve homemade food for lunch, and register students for your church's "adopt a student" program.

They're Adults

Involve committed Christians who are local college students on your church's teams and committees when possible. Invite the girls for ladies' retreat. Ask the guys to the men's golf tournament. Include them in choir, drama team, and mission projects. Invite them to sing a special song in worship.

Learn Their Names

Enough said.

International Students

Encourage church members to reach out to students from other countries. Families can "adopt" an international student at a local college and be a great encouragement to him or her. Many universities will help pair families with international students. The family can assist the student with English language, include the student in holiday celebrations, invite them for meals occasionally, help them with cultural adjustments, allow them to do their laundry at their home, and give them a taste of a home away from home. And more importantly, they can share Christ with the student!

Care Packages

A church group can send an occasional care package to out-of-town college students, praying for them as they prepare it.

- Carefully box homemade cookies in a Pringles can. Add a slice of bread to keep them fresh and a note challenging the student to share the cookies with new friends.
- Place an address label directly on a Crackerjacks or animal crackers box. Slip a note inside and use clear packing tape to seal it closed.
- During finals week, send a package of tea bags, colored pens, and a bookmark with Philippians 4:13.
- Ask church members to purchase $5 gift cards from fast-food establishments. Divide them between the college students and mail them with a greeting note.

Mail Matters

For a student away from home, mail is meaningful. Mail the weekly church bulletin or newsletter, clippings from the local newspaper, sermon CDs, and notes of encouragement.

Seven Days 'Til

Planning a high attendance for homecoming college students during a holiday break? Send a series of several postcards or notes, using a countdown.

- Two weeks 'til Thanksgiving Sunday. All college students Bible class at 9:00 a.m.
- One week 'til Thanksgiving Sunday. Can't wait to see you!
- Five days 'til Thanksgiving Sunday. Be there!

E-Scriptures

A leader in your church college Bible study could send a weekly Scripture to each college student from your church. No long note. Just an e-mail with "A Word from His Word" in the subject line and a carefully-chosen Scripture quoted in the text, every week for the entire school year.

Meet for Coffee or a Soft Drink

If business takes you near their college campus, arrange to meet them for coffee or a soft drink. They'll welcome a visit from their pastor, youth leader, Bible teacher, or friend. Especially if you buy them lunch!

Student Night at Christmas

It's an age-old tradition that's worth repeating. On Sunday evening after Christmas, students who have been away at college share testimonies of what God's been doing in their lives.

Let Them Go

Encourage college students to join a church in their new town and to get involved. They can join their home church again when they return. If they're home for the summer, help them find a place of ministry in the church. If they are considering serving as a summer missionary away from home, post regular updates about their ministry.

Community Outreach

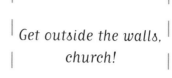

Get outside the walls, church!

"Go out into the highways and lanes and make them come in, so that my house may be filled."

—Luke 14:23

Need fresh ideas to touch the lost world that surrounds your church building?

Citywide Prayer Walk

Assign specific blocks in your community to different Sunday school classes, and simultaneously prayer walk the neighborhoods one day.

Power Lunch

Plan a weekly or monthly luncheon for local businessmen and women. Schedule luncheons on a specific day, such as the first Monday of each month or each Thursday from 11:45 to 12:30. Serve box lunches or hot lunch as they arrive. A speaker then relates Bible teaching to professional life, dismissing promptly as scheduled.

Farming

Draw a line on a map around an area in your community that your church would like to impact. It could be a new housing edition, a five-block radius of your church, or your entire town. This is your "farm" area. Call your denomination's state office to obtain demographics and research on the area. Make a list of every address in that area. Map out a three-year plan to impact each of those homes for Christ. Prayer walk. Leave a note card at each home committing to pray for them. Mail or deliver church newsletters, targeted brochures, or invitations to events. Observe carefully and attempt to meet needs. Share the gospel with every home during your three-year commitment. No immediate fruit? Keep on shining! Consider this: If you were unchurched and had received consistent, sincere contact from a local church, whom would you call in a crisis?

The World at Your Door

Here's a way to do foreign missions without crossing time zones or getting lots of shots. Internationals are moving to your town from around the world, many of them from countries that do not allow missionaries. International college students, families, and single adults are all a part of your church's local mission field. Find them. Welcome them. Help with furniture or friendship or cultural adjustments. Pair families with international students or families. And introduce them to a living God!

Library Ministry

Invite the community into your church building for a weekly story time for children. Advertise the story time in the local newspaper and the church bulletin. Deliver invitations to neighboring homes. Stake a sign on the church lawn. An animated reader can share stories from Christian books while parents browse the library and observe.

Neighborhood Coffee

Send invitations to invite every neighbor who lives near your church to a special Saturday morning coffee in their honor. Provide name tags and serve homemade snacks. Let them know that they are welcome at the church and that the church is available if they have an illness or a need. Invite them to use your church library and attend classes or worship. As they leave, present them with a gift, such as a coffee mug or magnet that says "ABC Baptist Church is praying for me" and lists church worship times and Web site. Give guests printed invitations to an upcoming children's event, topical Bible class, or special event.

Here's an Egg

Youth can help with this one! Deliver unique invitations for special events to the homes near your church. Deliver one plastic Easter egg containing an invitation to your annual kids' egg hunt. Deliver a small pumpkin with an invitation to Thanksgiving worship. Deliver a small flag with an invitation to July 4 celebration. They'll know you really want them to come.

Reverse Trick or Treat

Here's an outreach project for teens in your church. They prepare small bags of treats, including a church brochure and evangelistic tract. On Halloween night they blitz the community to deliver the bags to homes.

That High Grass across the Street

Don't complain about the church's neighborhood. Do something! Peeling paint at an elderly person's home? Your young adult Sunday school class can volunteer to paint for them. Unmowed lawn on a nearby vacant lot? Get permission to mow it.

Open Gym

If your church has a gymnasium, use it to impact the community. Policemen played basketball regularly in our church gym. Teens hung out there daily after school, and our youth minister and students played with them and shared Jesus. Local firemen used our church's exercise room regularly. Senior adults and young moms used the walking track regularly. Make a great effort to let them in instead of locking them out.

Shield a Badge with Prayer

Our church has implemented this plan for decades. It's simple but powerful. Obtain a list of police officers in your city, and ask individual church members to volunteer to pray for one officer for an entire year. They may send one or two notes annually to remind them that they are praying, but correspondence should be kept to a minimum and no special privilege expected. Print a bookmark for each praying member with the name of their assigned peace officer and a reminder to pray. Our church ordered a nice plaque: "First Baptist is praying today for our police department." The local police department hung it over their officers' entrance! See www.namb.net for detailed instructions.

Book for Peace

Purchase a specially printed Peace Officer's Bible or New Testament for each police officer in your city. The pastor may write a note in the front cover assuring them of the church's consistent prayers for them. Similarly, Bibles are printed for firefighters, congressional delegates, and military personnel.

New Mayor

When a new mayor, state representative, or other leader has been elected, purchase a personalized leather Bible as a gift for that leader. Make it more personal by asking all church members or church leaders to sign their names in the front cover.

English as a Second Language

What a gift! Help immigrants from around the world learn the language, and share Jesus while they're learning. Our church's ESL classes were scheduled on Wednesday so many church members who came for Wednesday evening dinner could easily attend the first ten minutes of the classes. Their responsibility was simply to converse casually with students before class began, aiding them in their conversation skills as they learned words. After the conversation minutes, those members left, and our ESL teachers led the class, using God's Word as part of their teaching.

Quill Ministry

Church members can write letters to public officials, police and fire departments, and local school administration to let them know that your church is praying for them.

Neighborly Niceties

It's easy to overlook opportunities to show God's love to businesses nearby your church building. A church member or staff member could write a note each year to ask if the church can help them in any way, to compliment an improvement to their building or success in their business, or to promise to pray for them. "Love your neighbor" includes them too!

Community Publications

Place advertisements about your church in local school football or basketball programs, theater playbills, Little League calendars, etc. Consider the target audience and design the ad to impact them. For example, a high school football ad could spotlight a photo of your church teens at summer camp and an invitation to after-game youth fellowships at your church. A theater program could advertise your church's annual pageant or a worship service that includes a dramatic skit.

Media Coverage

For large church events and unique ministries, notify local media. The local television, radio, or newspaper may cover the story. Send high-quality digital photographs along with a brief description and contact information. Always send a thank-you note to the editor or producer when your church is mentioned in the media.

Creative Arts

Encourage artists to use their gifts in church.

"I have filled him with God's Spirit, with wisdom, understanding, and ability in every craft to design artistic works . . ."

—Exodus 31:3–4

It's one of the most overlooked and underused means of sharing Christ. Need fresh ideas to encourage creative arts in your church?

Creativity Welcome!

His sky is the limit to ways the arts can be used to praise and serve God in the local church. Mime, photography, sculpting, puppets, interpretive movement, videography, clowning, woodcarving, quilting, costume design, metalwork, needlepoint, media arts, vocal music, instrumental music, poetry—the list could go on and on. Whatever artistic gift God has given his people can be used to his glory. Encourage artistic expression in your church.

Art Exhibit

Plan an annual Christian art exhibit at your church. Announce it several months ahead, inviting artists to submit original art. All submissions should have a Christian theme. Select a theme Scripture annually, such as Proverbs 3:5–6, or a theme topic, such as "God cares." The exhibit can incorporate all mediums of art, from canvas to sculpture to jewelry. Use tripods, pillars, trophy cases, and tables to display the art in one central area and recruit art-loving, God-loving volunteers to greet guests. Arrange benches and chairs for relaxed viewing, and play soft Christian music during the art show. Advertise the exhibit to the community and the church, and send special invitations to art-related businesses and art teachers in the area. At a pre-event reception for participating artists, pray that God will use their art to touch lives.

Simultaneous Sermon Art

Add impact to a themed sermon with this awesome idea. An artist paints an entire work of art during a special song or during a sermon. The artist must carefully time the project exactly to fit the audio message. I've seen this done with chalk art, watercolors on an enormous canvas, and paints on a huge Plexiglas. Very effective.

Summer Arts Program

If your church is blessed with gifted artists, consider planning a summer arts program for children or adults. A fee may be charged to cover art supplies. Lessons could be offered along with a strong Christian witness.

All-Day VBS and Art

Wouldn't working parents love to bring their child to an all-day program? Your church could schedule Vacation Bible School in the morning and artistic classes in the afternoons.

Original Art

Invite artists in the church to submit original Christian art for use on church bulletins, newsletters, bookmarks, and event programs. Need a logo for a church camp or ministry? Ask an artist in your church. For example, an artist in our church designed a logo for our women's ministry. She drew a rendering of a stained glass at our church with two joined hands. The logo was used in various formats for every women's ministry event.

Drama Team

A quality drama team can bring a sermon theme to life with a brief dramatic sketch during worship. If a pastor plans sermons topics in advance or preaches a series, a drama group can prepare effective vignettes to enhance the theme. Some churches use a familiar cast of characters repeatedly; others vary their presentations dramatically. In our church dramatic skits were usually between two and four minutes long. Add variety with dramatic readings, signing, interpretive movement, or mime. Street drama sketches are effective in many missions settings and community fairs. Use drama. It touches hearts.

Theater Arts

A gifted drama teacher in our church helped our teens plan an annual summer dinner theater with a full-length evangelistic Christian drama. The play was selected to impact lost friends for Christ. (Two great scripts: *Three in One** and *Catacombs*. The students created elaborate backdrops and sets, perfected the presentation, and presented multiple sold-out performances annually. (*Order from www.tledford@prodigy.net.)

Architectural Feature

What is the most attractive feature of your church building? Maybe it's a gorgeous stained-glass window or a steeple. Perhaps it's the front view of the entrance or the pulpit or the sanctuary. Maybe your church building is gorgeous from an aerial view or a distant photo shot. Carefully consider the most enticing physical element and ask a photographer to capture it using a flattering angle. An exterior shot may be more inviting with lots of people entering. Use the photo on bulletins, business cards, note cards, postcards, brochures, and advertisements. Alternately, an artist in your church may draw a rendering of the feature. Our church used the architectural feature as a background for sermon PowerPoint presentations.

Focal Art

For a special event at your church, invite an artist to create a huge focal backdrop on canvas. A church motto. A revival theme. A missions challenge. An annual theme or Scripture.

Talking Sidewalks

Artistic teens can multiply a sermon's impact with colorful sidewalk art. Using chalk, they sketch words and art to remind worshippers of a key sermon phrase or topic for a special sermon. For example, the sermon title is "Yes, Lord!" Teens write that phrase all around the church on the walkways, and every worshipper not only hears the sermon but walks on it!

Raise Your Banner High

Elaborate or simple banners can add style, color, and focus. They can be permanently hung in your church sanctuary, foyers, or atriums. Banners can be temporarily displayed for a special sermon theme or musical or season. They can be carried in on poles as part of a dramatic reading or theatrical event. Informal banners could be spaced around a gymnasium walking track. Banners can be small or huge, square or oblong, ornate or contemporary. *The only real rule is this: Banners must point the viewer to God.* Hope Community Church, Brownsburg, Indiana, has six entire unique sets of contemporary banners for their worship center—one for each season of the year. A team of artistic women in our church created many gorgeous banners—an elaborate Christian wedding banner, Christmas banners, Easter, Lord's Supper, and dozens of banners to illustrate the names of God.

The Potter's Wheel

Want to leave worshippers thinking about a sermon about God as our maker? A potter's wheel is set up at the side of the stage area of worship. A potter silently and thoughtfully forms and completes a lovely piece of pottery while the sermon is preached or a fitting song is sung.

Kiln for Christ

Does your church have a ceramics kiln or gifted ceramic artists? Our church ceramics team created personalized baby gifts for each new baby born to a church member or friend or relative of church members. That team made gifts for the church's community welcome team, homebound member gifts, and hospital visitation teams.

Second Bloom

A team of women arrived early for our weekly church's ladies day. They took flowers from Sunday's worship flower arrangements and made several small arrangements for delivery to hospitals during ministry time. Ladies bought inexpensive vases by the dozens at garage sales to use for this project.

Daylight Savings Time

"Joshua prayed to the LORD in front of all the people of Israel. He said, 'Let the sun stand still.'"

—Josh 10:12 (NLT)

Plan ahead to capitalize on daylight savings time Sunday. Need fresh ideas?

Spring Forward Ideas

Free Wakeup Calls

One time-change Sunday morning our church's fifth graders gave friendly wakeup calls to their classmates and had an all-time high attendance. With prior planning you could ask church members to register to receive a "free" Sunday wakeup call on daylight savings Sunday.

Remember. Remember. Remember.

Losing an hour on spring's daylight savings Sunday can hurt attendance, so use every means to remind folks. Announce it on your church Web site. Print it in the church newsletter and bulletin. Send a mass e-mail to church members on Saturday to remind them to change their clocks. Use a phone tree recording to call members automatically on Saturday to remind them.

Oops!

It's inevitable that a few stragglers will accidentally arrive at church just before worship is over, embarrassed that they forgot the time change. Ushers should rope off rear pews and be readily available to seat them unobtrusively. Ushers can give latecomers a note stating that a complimentary CD or tape recording of the service will be available for them immediately following the service.

Fall Back Ideas

Really High

That extra hour of sleep for the fall time change makes it an ideal day for a high-attendance emphasis such as No Excuse Sunday, When the Role Is Called Up Yonder, or Really High Attendance Sunday.

It's a Sign

The exterior church sign could read, "You get an extra hour Sunday morning. See you in church!"

Early Rise? Advertise!

This would be an excellent week to place an ad in your local newspaper to invite newcomers to church.

"Glad Ya Came Early"

Early birds who forget to change their clocks will arrive an hour early. Plan to greet them well. A large sign near entrances can read, "Glad you came early today!" and offer some upbeat options:

- Our church library is open early today. Stop by!
- Take time for early morning prayer in our sanctuary this morning. (Play taped music.)
- Enjoy coffee and doughnuts in the fellowship hall this morning. Place a dish of gummy worms on the table with a fun sign, "The early bird gets the worm! Glad you're here."

Welcome to Sunday School

Some who don't usually attend Bible classes may accidentally arrive in time for Sunday school, so greeters must be prepared to escort them to a quality class.

Deacon Ordination

Celebrate servant leaders.

"Select from among you . . . men of good reputation, full of the Spirit and wisdom, whom we can appoint to this duty."

—Acts 6:3

Plan a special ceremony to appoint servant leaders for your church. Need fresh ideas?

Invitations

Print invitations to the deacon ordination service for the new deacon to mail to friends and relatives.

Be There!

Use a photograph of the new deacon in your Sunday morning preservice audio-visual announcements, encouraging church members to attend the upcoming deacon ordination.

Testimony

The person being ordained as a deacon could give his salvation testimony and share what it means to him to be invited to serve as a deacon in the church.

Take Up Your Towel

Present each new deacon with a simple white hand towel, or order imprinted towels. Use John 13 as you formally present a towel to each new deacon as an acknowledgement of servant leadership.

Autographs

Before the service begins, request that each ordained minister and ordained deacon attending the service write their name on the back of the deacon ordination certificate. Or present a Bible with the signatures of ordained ministers and deacons inside the front cover.

My Husband's a Deacon

Honor the new deacon's wife by presenting her a flower and a book about deacon wives. Recognize family and extended family members of the new deacon by asking them to stand.

Badge of Honor

Present new deacons with a deacon lapel pin.

Pillows

At the conclusion of the church's ordination service for deacons, all ordained deacons and ministers may be invited to come to the front of the sanctuary, encircle the new deacons, lay hands on them, and say a prayer for them. A member of our church even made small kneeling pillows just for this ceremony.

New Deacon Reception

After the ordination service, invite all those present to attend a nice reception in honor of the new deacons and their families. Form a receiving line with the new deacons and their spouse and/or family.

Easter

The biggest Sunday of the year!

"Keep in mind Jesus Christ, risen from the dead."

—2 Timothy 2:8

There's no better holiday to tell a lost world about a risen Savior! Need fresh ideas?

Palm Branches

Order palm branches from a local florist, and allow older children to form two lines outside at the entrances to create a pathway for church attenders. Children can wave the palm branches and joyfully shout "hosanna" as church members arrive on Palm Sunday. Some churches even use a donkey to reenact Palm Sunday!

A Different Kind of Crown

Ask a creative person in your church to make a simple "crown of thorns" centerpiece for the sanctuary on Easter Sunday.

Easter Lilies

Does your church traditionally decorate the sanctuary with dozens of Easter lilies on resurrection Sunday? Make assignments for deacons to deliver lilies to homebound members on Easter afternoon.

An Amazing Good Friday Service

It lasts less than an hour and features seven sermons by seven preachers. Six preachers (guest pastors, staff members, or seminary professors) are each assigned one of the seven last phrases that Jesus spoke from the cross and the task of preparing a striking five-minute sermon about that phrase. Your church's pastor will preach about the last phrase. After a reverent song and Lord's Supper observance, lights are dimmed, leaving only the podium light and seven lit candles at the front. Introduction of speakers is printed rather than voiced. Speakers approach sequentially to dynamically share, in less than five minutes each, the seven last phrases our Christ spoke as he died on the cross for our sins. After preaching, each preacher blows out one candle. As the last candle is snuffed, the auditorium is left briefly in total darkness. (Quite symbolic.) The pastor simply states, "And he died." As lights begin to come back up, he reminds the congregation that this is not the end of the account and invites them back on Easter Sunday to hear the rest of the story.

Sunrise Celebration

Schedule an outdoor sunrise service exactly at sunrise on Easter Sunday morning. Just imagine the surprise and joy of discovering an empty tomb on Easter morning, and convey that joy through a brief and informal celebration.

"There Was Nowhere to Park"

"So I just went back home." When an unsaved friend made that comment after a packed-out Easter service, our church made a new plan. On high-attendance Sundays, we offered off-site parking for members who cared enough to leave room for guests, and we shuttled them to the door.

Butter Lambs

Plan a class at church to teach how to make butter lambs for Easter dinner. Each person brings a pound of butter and two dishes. Participants make two lambs, one for their own Easter dinner and another for a friend. The teacher shares how the "Lamb of God" was sacrificed on the first Easter. Instructions for butter lambs are easily found on the Internet.

Egg Hunt

An egg hunt on Saturday before Easter can be a great outreach event. Put invitations to the hunt inside plastic eggs for all members to give to neighbors and friends. Ask families to bring a dozen eggs for each child. Carefully mark boundaries, allowing separate hunting grounds for younger children. Hundreds of eggs are prehidden, along with prize eggs. As guests arrive, moms and children have fun creating with sidewalk chalk or blowing bubbles while dads and older kids hide eggs. The actual hunt lasts only minutes. After the hunt, present a five-minute program telling the Easter story of resurrection in a creative way, then award prizes and serve snacks. Church members can fellowship with guests and personally invite them to Bible study and worship on Sunday.

E-mail

"And this news spread throughout that whole area."

—Matthew 9:26

It's like mail, without a stamp. Need fresh ideas?

E-Invitations

One of the best methods of inviting unchurched guests is to create an e-invitation, e-mail it to members, and request that they forward it to friends. Create an e-invitation specifically designed to invite friends for Bible study, worship, baptism, special events, Vacation Bible School, or revival.

E-Newsletter

Many churches e-mail their biweekly or monthly church newsletter directly to members and other interested people.

I Don't Do E-Mail

If your church newsletter is sent only by e-mail, offer occasional lessons for members who don't use computers. A computer may be set up in the church library for members' use, or most public libraries offer Internet use.

Weekly E-Update

Send a weekly announcement page to each church member with an e-mail address. It's free, simple, and effective.

Sunday School/Small Group E-Ministry

Without exception every growing Sunday school department I've visited lately uses e-mail effectively. Publish a list of class member e-mail addresses to encourage fellowship. Sending weekly class updates is very effective, and the list of effective uses is limitless. Some suggestions:

- Sunday's attendance numbers
- New members introduction—Print new members' contact information and their Christian testimony or a well-written introduction.
- Sunday's guests' names and e-mail contact
- Personal touches, such as birthdays, anniversaries, praises, prayer requests
- Report of last week's church and class activities
- Detailed announcement of next week's events
- Dates of future events
- Scripture—possibly verses for sermon text or Bible lesson next week

Predictable Is Good

Send your church or class e-update every Tuesday. Or the first day of every month. A predictable, consistent e-update will be anticipated and read.

Short, Sweet, and Upbeat

Ensure that every word of your church or class e-mail update is worth reading. Remember this: Short and sweet is a real treat; rambling and long? They'll hit "delete." Write, then rewrite. Use photos, charts, and stats to add interest.

Subject Line

Always use a consistent subject line title for weekly class or church e-mails, i.e. "Koinonia Class Communiqué" or "First Baptist E-Blessings."

Urgent E-mails

In addition to regular e-announcements, a special e-alert may be sent for significant announcements such as a large church event, daylight savings time reminder, crisis or disaster details. Again, use a consistent subject line for these more urgent communications, i.e. "First Baptist E-Alert" or "Koinonia Class Urgent Update."

Link It

Each class update or church e-mail note should include a link to the church Web site.

Aunt Jewel's Ingrown Toenail

If your church's e-update includes lists of prayer requests, be careful to avoid privacy infringement and overinformation. God knows the details.

Event
Evangelism

"'Follow Me,' He told them, 'and I will make
you fish for people!'"

—Matthew 4:19

Don't sit inside the church walls and wait for the world to knock. Get out!

First-Place Float

Design and create a fabulous float for your town's annual parade. You'll find that almost any parade theme can be pointed toward God! Ask an artistic church member to design a top-quality entry. It will take dozens of hard-working church members to make a quality float, but your church will be exposed to many lost people. Add walkers beside the float to distribute unique invitations to an upcoming event at your church.

Unique Parade Performance

It's a fun way to get a presence in the town's parade. A group of teens, adults, or children form a precision rhythm team to march and perform in the town's parade. Their formation is military. Their movements are sharp and precise. And the overall performance points to God. For example, teens could perform a funky well-rehearsed "sticks" routine, using dowel rods to do a rhythm routine to illustrate a contemporary Christian song. How about a choreographed kids' or adults' kazoo band or a mom's stroller squad? A Bible "drill team" could all wear white clothes, dark glasses, carry large black Bibles and march to a cadence. Their precision footwork and hand motions point the viewer to the Word, and they could occasionally stop and rhythmically recite a Scripture.

They'll steal the show! Guys from your church's weekly businessmen's Bible lunch could form a "briefcase brigade." They all wear black suits, matching ties, and black sunglasses and carry black briefcases with a cross on both sides. Extra men walk alongside to distribute invitations to the men's Bible study. Parades are for fun. Share some Christian joy!

A Cup of Water

Does your community have an annual festival? Get visible! Set up a stage and share quality Christian music, using various ensembles, individuals, and choirs from your church. Or wear church T-shirts, pull a wagon full of iced water, carry a "free water" sign, and pass out bottled water and church brochures. Rent a prime-location booth for a unique purpose that can be used to share Christ. Some examples: free temporary cross tattoos or face paint can be applied while you share a witness and a tract. Free hot chocolate or soft drinks could be distributed along with an invitation to an event at your church. Order inexpensive handouts, personalized for your church. Choose something usable or eye-catching, such as plastic fans or cool foam hats. Helium balloons with a printed invitation to your church will create walking advertisements. If weather will likely be hot for the festival, rent or make a mister. As people walk through to cool off, a sign reads, "Worship at First Baptist Church is even more refreshing than this! See you Sunday!"

High-Flying Tradition

Begin a new citywide tradition on your church property. Plan a huge kite-flying contest on the first day of spring every year. Or declare a huge snowman-building contest for adults, teens, and kids on the first snow holiday each year. Take lots of photographs and invite guests to church on Sunday to see the photos.

Let's Do Lunch

Our quarterly church's ladies luncheons were one of our church's largest and most effective evangelism events. The decorations were gorgeous, and the glitz and high-energy atmosphere created an unintimidating opportunity to share Jesus with friends. The program featured great music and an inspirational speaker and was timed precisely to fit the weekday lunch hour so working women could attend. Members planned ahead to invite new acquaintances and unsaved friends. We advertised in local newspapers, and ladies came from all over town. The door-prize entry forms obtain contact information for follow-up, and women are invited to mark a star on the form if they want to learn more about becoming a Christian or joining the church.

Citywide Fishing Contest

Is there a pond or lake near your church? Plan a citywide kids' fishing contest, complete with casting lessons, participation certificates, and grandmas delivering lemonade for fisher-kids. Present trophies or ribbons for biggest fish, smallest fish, most fish, best technique, and sportsmanship award. Order brightly colored visors or caps with the church logo. Invite every family to worship on Sunday to see fishing photos and a sermon tied to fishing.

Free Walk-In Movie on Church Lawn

Invite the community to see a family movie or a major sports event projected on a big blank exterior wall of your church. Advertise it well, asking folks to bring blankets and lawn chairs. Provide free popcorn and sodas. Laugh, have fun, and meet strangers in a relaxed setting. Announce that photos of the evening will be shown on video projection on Sunday.

Join Us!

At every outdoor evangelism event, display a large church banner that shouts "welcome!" so the community will know they're invited to join in.

Outdoor (or Indoor) Christian Music Concert

Invite the community to a Christian concert, featuring a great Christian singing group or your own church youth band. Advertise a free concert, set up a stage, a great sound system, and chairs for twice as many people as you expect.

Worship in the Grass

Does your church have a nice, lush lawn? Plan an outdoor worship service, a volleyball tournament, an Easter egg hunt, or a homemade ice cream party. Use it for a kids' Christian soccer league or youth flag football league.

Block Parties Work

Hundreds of block parties were planned all around Indianapolis during the Crossover evangelistic emphasis before the Southern Baptist Convention was in our town. Every one of the block parties was a whopping success! Many associations of churches have block party trailers for their churches' use.

Who's the Guest?

At a large outdoor church event, it may be hard to distinguish guests from members. Put stick-on dots on members' clothing. It works beautifully.

Fall Festival

"Let the little children come to Me."

—Mark 10:14

Many churches seek to provide a safe alternative at Halloween by having a fall festival for kids.

Costume Parade

Plan a costume parade in your church parking lot for the whole community. Rent a huge balloon animal to place outside your church to invite the community to participate. Rope off the parade route safely and designate a staging area. The pastor could lead the parade on a go-cart, carrying a sign that says, "Jesus Loves the Little Children" on one side, and "So does our church!" on the back. In the staging area children can practice waving and walking in a unique way to match their costumes. Space children individually or in twos so viewers can see them. Friendly church members could distribute witnessing tracts designed for the occasion, and children's Sunday school teachers could pass out invitations for Sunday. The last costumed person in the parade could carry this sign: "If you think this was exciting, wait 'til you come to church on Sunday!" Use lots of balloons and confetti, and distribute free hot chocolate.

Festival Photos

Turn your fall festival into an outreach. Display a large "free photo!" sign at the entrance next to a beautiful photo spot you've prepared using colorful leaves, mums, pumpkins, and hay. Recruit photo buffs in your church to bring tripods and 35mm or digital cameras (not Polaroid). Recruit a child-loving, friendly church member to assist with cute poses. Working quickly to avoid lines, take one shot of each child who attends the festival. Give parents a printed note to pick up their child's photo in the church foyer on Sunday. Your entire church will enjoy the photos, and members and guests may pick up photos after worship. Deliver guests' photos that are not picked up.

Registration

A quick and simple registration process at your church's Fall Festival can obtain important contact information. When families register, give them free tickets for entrance, tickets for door prizes, or tickets for individual booths.

Pumpkin Fest

Many church festivals offer carnival-type games, clowns, bounce-house, mazes made of boxes for preschoolers, tractor rides, face painting, live Christian music, a cupcake walk, and great food. Some churches charge a nominal fee for snacks. Each adult Bible class in our church planned a game booth to fit our festival theme each year. Annual themes could be Noah's Ark, Kids in the Bible, Animals in the Bible, or Famous Bible Heroes.

Trunk or Treat

As another alternative to Halloween, church members park their cars all around the church parking lot with trunks facing the center. Church members can decorate their trunks, wear costumes if they want to, and pass out candy to children. Be sure to distribute evangelistic tracts and a written and verbal invitation to church next Sunday.

Nursing Home Parade

Work with a local nursing home director to plan a special treat for their residents. Children from your church meet at the front entrance wearing costumes and parade through the nursing home hallways, waving at residents and distributing candies and evangelistic tracts.

Little Bo Peep on Skates

If your church has a gym or outdoor space, you could plan a costume party on skates. Play kids' Christian music, and invite the community.

Reverse Trick or Treat

It's the one night of the year that folks are glad to answer the door. Members of your church go door-to-door to distribute small bags that contain a witnessing tract, a pencil with the church name, a printed magnet that says, "Our church is praying for you," and an invitation to church.

Father's Day

Don't celebrate
Mother's Day and
ignore Father's Day.

*"Sons are indeed a heritage from the LORD, children,
a reward. . . . Happy is the man who has filled
his quiver with them."*

—Psalms 127:3, 5

Need fresh ideas to make Father's Day significant?

Me and Dad Slide Show

Ask members to submit one photograph of themselves with their dad. Create a touching slide show, accompany it with an appropriate Christian song, and show it during the offertory on Father's Day.

My Dad's the Greatest

Create a montage of five-second video testimonies by kids of all ages in your church, completing this sentence: My Dad's the greatest because . . .

Annual Father/Child Event

Begin a new tradition in your church that involves fathers. It could be a father/child kickball game or fishing trip or a father/daughter tea. Allow children without fathers to "borrow" a church member who has no children for the event.

Gift Ideas

If your church likes to give a gift on Father's Day, consider a book, a fish hook lapel pin, a music CD, or a bookmark with Scriptures about fathers. Purchase books about Christian fathers in bulk. An older children's class could make simple boutonnieres or your church could order them from a florist.

Fellowship

There's nothing quite like fellowship among Christians.

"They gave the right hand of fellowship to me."

—Galatians 2:9

The world should look at your church and observe joyful relationships. Need some fresh ideas?

That's Me Up There!

Take lots of digital photos of members participating in church ministries and events and project them as part of the preservice audiovisual. People will get to know one another, and members of all ages will be delighted to see themselves "caught" serving or fellowshipping together. And there's an additional benefit: guests will observe Christian joy and friendship.

Pictorial Directories

With digital cameras it's easier than ever to keep up-to-date photos of church members. Whether you produce it in-house or use a photo company, keep an updated church directory. Nothing helps a new member more.

My Church Mail

Some churches build a wall of mail slots for every church family. Members check their mailbox often to pick up church newsletters, personal notes, and contribution envelopes. The mail wall also provides a visual reminder when a member hasn't attended lately.

Pray for Me Today

A prayer calendar, mailed as part of your church newsletter, could remind members to pray for one another. Use a one-month calendar page, and on each day of the month, list one church member or family's name, one church staff member or leader's name, and one specific ministry of the church. Wouldn't you be honored to have your entire church praying for you today?

Church Bumper Stickers

Order classy or clever bumper stickers for old and new church members. You'll be amazed at how it helps people recognize one another and offers simple witnessing opportunities.

E-mail Updates

Fellowship is increased when church members are informed about church ministries and activities. Create a database of e-mail addresses of church members who have them, then send weekly e-mail updates.

Church T-shirts

When printing T-shirts for church events, sports, or groups, always include the church name on them. Members become a walking billboard to invite lost people to church. What a simple way to be a witness!

Pitch In or Pot Luck

Here's an important rule for carry-in dinners: serve from two sides of the table. Create separate serving areas for drinks and for desserts to help with flow.

Every Week Fellowship

First Southern Baptist Church of Evansville has had an all-church fellowship almost every Sunday evening after worship for thirty-three years! Pastor Don Moore attributes the church's steady growth and sweet harmony to that consistent weekly time of informal snacks and relaxed Christian fellowship.

Summer Nights

Do those who hang around on Sunday evenings after worship often end up meeting at a restaurant for snacks? Just a little planning can help include everyone and increase fellowship. Ask six hospitable church members if they will host a casual backyard gathering one Sunday evening this summer. Backyard fellowships would be perfect! Choose six Sunday evenings during the summer, and announce to the evening crowd that they're all invited for snacks and fellowship right after church.

Rare Talent Competition

Serve rare meats (such as buffalo, duck, venison), "uncooked" tossed salad, undercooked baked potatoes, unusual condiments and side dishes, and a rare dessert of some kind. Several weeks before the Rare Talent Party, recruit several contenders to begin the competition signup, asking each class or group in the church to enter at least one competitor. Each contender will demonstrate a unique "talent," anything from picking up items with toes to quoting the ABCs backward to a kazoo duet. Make a crazy trophy by mounting an unusual item on a piece of wood for the first-prize winner.

Don't Rush Home

Here's one of the most inviting fellowship ideas I've seen lately. Calvary Baptist in West Lafayette, Indiana, demolished two pint-sized classrooms which were located adjacent to the church foyer. A church member designed and built the classiest coffee-shop fellowship area you can imagine. It has rich woods, comfy furniture, flat-screen television with closed circuit of worship service, and coffee and cappuccino machines. The area is open to the church foyer, and it invites before and after-church fellowship. It's a perfect place for discipleship, too. Caring volunteers serve drinks an hour before and after each worship service.

Just Do It

Fellowship is critical to a Sunday school class or church. Think of any excuse for a time of fellowship with church members! Some examples:

- Milk and Cookies Fellowship
- New Year's Brunch
- All-church Picnic
- Garden Party
- "Low" Tea (instead of high)
- Game Night
- Cookout
- A Day at the Lake
- Backyard Campout
- Lottie Moon Auction Party
- Bowling or miniature golf or volleyball tournament
- Flashlight Easter Egg Hunt (adults or youth)
- Hat Party
- Christmas Caroling Party
- Food contest, i.e. chili, cakes, homemade ice cream
- House Slipper Tea
- Welcome fellowship to honor new church members
- Roller Skate Party for all ages
- Sports competition

Graduation

*"For I know the plans I have for you . . . to give you
a future and a hope."*

—Jeremiah 29:11

Send those high school graduates off with your church's blessings. Need fresh ideas?

Sealed "Blessing Book"

Begin early to complete this simple but meaningful project to celebrate high school graduation. Purchase a bottle of rubber cement and a nice journal with lined pages for each high school graduate from your church. Write the graduate's name on the front of the journal, and a note, "Do not open until 2013!" (four years from now). Pass the book around to youth leaders, church staff members, and other church friends of the graduate. Each person writes a personal note on a separate page with this in mind: the graduate can't read the note for four years! They may share words of Christian encouragement, Scriptures, observations of spiritual gifts, funny or serious predictions, notes of love or prayers. After each person writes his or her note, they seal their page closed using rubber cement. My daughter just opened her blessing book after four years of college. What a blessing it was! The notes were convicting, hilarious, challenging, touching.

And the Graduates Are . . .

Make bookmarks with a list of your church's high school graduates and a challenge to pray for them. Print them on cardstock paper and laminate. Distribute the prayer reminders to church members on Sunday.

Testimony

Graduates' Christian testimonies could be printed as a bulletin insert.

Senior Wall

Take an annual group photo of your church's grads on graduate recognition Sunday. Pose the group uniquely each year, i.e. leaning, walking in line, on playground equipment. Let the group choose a Scripture to add to the bottom of the photo, then frame it and hang it on the "senior wall" in the church's youth area.

Projected Pictures

Preservice video projection could feature a baby photo and cap and gown photo of each graduate along with a challenge to the church to pray for graduates. It could also include a quote by a youth worker or staff member about that student's spiritual walk during the past years or a quote by the graduate about his or her relationship with God.

Stand Up

When introducing graduates during worship, ask church members who have invested in that student to stand, such as family members, past Sunday school teachers, church youth workers.

Graduate Commissioning

Some churches honor graduates with a brief ceremony during worship. Graduates wear their caps and gowns and are seated on the front rows. They are introduced with a sentence about their Christian walk. After all graduates have been introduced, invite parents to come forward to stand with their graduate for a special prayer of commitment and commissioning. Youth workers should pray with students whose parents aren't present. Read Matthew 28:18–20 as a challenge. Allow a time for parents and friends to pray quietly with their student before the group prays together. Conclude with a pastoral prayer, commissioning the students to impact their world.

Thanks a Bunch

At the graduate recognition service, present each graduate with a sunflower or daisy as they're introduced. After all have been introduced, invite them to take the flower to an adult in the congregation who has been a Christian encourager to them.

Receiving Lines

After the worship service where graduates are recognized, ask graduates to form a line in the church foyer or hallway so members may offer words of encouragement to them.

Visual Story

The youth minister or parents may prepare a video or slide show of the students at church activities over the years and share it during a special fellowship gathering. A party for the entire group of graduates from your church could spotlight each student with a poster, prepared by their parents. Give parents plenty of advance notice, requesting that the poster be submitted a couple of weeks early. The poster could portray the graduate from infancy through graduation.

Breakfast for Grads

Plan a special event to honor your church's high school graduates—a casual reception, an outdoor barbeque, a formal tea party, a photo party, or a huge banquet. Our church hosted a lovely breakfast for graduates and their families on the Sunday morning of graduate recognition. Graduates shared testimonies of what the church had meant to them and their future plans. Youth leaders led concluding prayers for the graduates.

Bible Gift

A friend of mine bought a nice "Share Jesus without Fear" New Testament for his son's graduation gift. The month before graduation, he asked many church leaders, staff, deacons, and youth workers to highlight one inspiring Scripture and write their name and a brief encouragement note in the margin beside it.

Light Your World

If your church presents a gift to graduating seniors, select a gift that will encourage their Christian walk. Order personalized flashlights for each graduate, imprinted with their names and Matthew 5:14a, 16b. Other ideas: Scripture magnet, Christian bookstore gift certificate, study Bible signed by church leaders, an appropriate Christian book.

Greeters

"And if you greet only your brothers, what are you doing out of the ordinary?"

—Matthew 5:47

Practice hospitality at church. Need fresh ideas?

Identifiable

Greeters should wear something to identify them as a person in charge so guests will be more comfortable asking questions or directions. Some churches use greeter badges or name tags. Others order matching polo shirts. Greeters at one church wear matching maroon jackets.

One Greeting Is Not Enough

An elderly gentleman at a church explained to me that he was "greeter 2 at door 3." It was not a huge church, but his weekly responsibility was to stand just inside one entrance to the worship center, and after greeter 1 gave the bulletin, he welcomed each person. It's not overkill; it's called *greeting*. At key entrances to worship, consider this double-greet method.

The Umbrella Squad

Assign a separate team of men and women from one of your church's young adult Bible classes as the church umbrella squad. Purchase huge golf umbrellas and store them in a closet. Anytime there is a rainy Sunday or a sudden downpour during worship, they spring into action, escorting worshippers to their cars and perhaps even valeting cars for elderly folks.

More than Bulletin Distribution

Greeters can direct cars into parking lots, greet outdoors near the first-time guest parking spots, open car doors at entrances, greet members and guests in foyers and worship entries, assist parents with small children, help lost people get found, walk guests to Bible classrooms, give directions, and distribute bulletins. It's an important responsibility. Keep a list of substitutes so volunteers can be sure their position is covered during vacations or emergencies.

Looking Good. Smelling Good.

Impressions made during a guest's first seconds are hard to reverse. Greeters must make a positive first impression with their appearance, personality, eye contact, and manners. He or she must be clean, modestly dressed, and well-groomed. A breath mint wouldn't hurt, either!

Different and Alike

Greeters can be longtime church members and brand new Christians. Use greeters who vary in age, marital status, ethnicity, and gender. Consider using a married couple at one door and single adults at another. A friendly teen may greet with a senior adult. Parents may greet with their child. But the common denominator is this: greeters should be some of the warmest, friendliest, most God-loving members of your church.

Is This Sunday?

How disconcerting it is for a guest to arrive to an empty foyer or cavernous sanctuary! Guests often arrive at a time when most people are in a Bible class. Be certain a friendly greeter is always ready to welcome guests at the door. The worship center is more inviting if soft recorded or live music is playing and audiovisual announcements are running. Begin them at least a half hour before worship time.

Greeters' Gala

Make it a privilege to be on the greeter team by planning an annual fellowship. A Christmas party, summer picnic, or chili party for greeters and their families will enhance their fellowship with one another.

The Welcome Center

A Welcome Center in a central location at your church can provide materials, directions, and information for guests. Many churches build custom half-circle counters for a classy-looking greeter center. Carefully plan your guest registration process so it's quick and easy. Some churches serve coffee and pastries while guests register. Each guest should be personally escorted to their Sunday school classroom and introduced to someone there. If the guest has a child, take the child to class first so the parents can see their classroom and know where to retrieve their child. Each Sunday afternoon, greeters at the welcome center should write a personal note to each guest they welcome.

Greet Them "Good-bye"

It's not over until it's over. Station a greeter at each exit to greet everyone "good-bye".

Groundbreaking

It's a groundbreaking event!

"I will thank the LORD with all my heart; I will declare all Your wonderful works."

—**Psalm 9:1**

Breaking ground for a new church building? Some celebration ideas:

Bless This Dirt

If your church just bought property for a new church location, plan an informal dedication prayer time immediately after the land purchase is finalized. Invite all church members to gather on the vacant property, kneel, and dedicate the site to God.

A Groundbreaking Event

Just before construction begins for your church building, plan a groundbreaking celebration. Call it "A Groundbreaking Event."

Banner Invitation

Carefully choose the most visible location on the property, and install a professionally painted banner or sign to let the community know that your church is building there. Personalize the words to the community, i.e. "Building a family life center to impact Tanglewood for Christ." Invite readers to join the group for worship at the current location. Place a notification about the groundbreaking event on the sign diagonally at least a week before the celebration.

Official Announcements

Mail a press release about the groundbreaking ceremony to each local newspaper and radio station. For the newspapers, include a photo of the vacant property with a banner about the groundbreaking, a rendering of the proposed building, and a photograph of the pastor.

Invitations

Send printed or computer-generated invitations to local officials, such as the mayor, asking them to RSVP and arrive a few minutes early for special seating. Invitations may also be mailed to recent visitors to your church as well as the building contractor for the project. If your church is a mission church, print an invitation in the parent church's newsletter, and be certain that that pastor is part of the program.

Something's Happening Here!

Hang pennant-style flags to attract attention. Or rent a couple of really high-flying balloons or wiggly balloon-guys so passersby will know it's a special day. Or if you have a small-plane pilot in your church, how about arranging a flyby with a trailing banner?

Shades of Purple

It will assist with planning if you select a color scheme for a groundbreaking event. For example, if you choose a lime green and lemon yellow color scheme, then balloons, table coverings, flags, flowers, and invitations may be selected to fit the color scheme. Color planning adds class and interest to the event.

A Balloon Archway

Create a focal point for the groundbreaking ceremony by using a portable stage, a balloon archway, or a tent. Set up a few dozen chairs near the stage, leaving room for the shovel ceremony. Chairs should be well marked for visiting dignitaries with a few extras for elderly people. Most attenders will simply stand for the brief ceremony. Since the ceremony will be short, this will add excitement and seem like an even larger crowd. A separate stage area should be set up for the musicians.

Golden Shovels

Spray-paint several shovels shiny gold or fluorescent green or whatever color you prefer. Prepare a shovel for each person who will participate in the shovel ceremony, such as pastor, deacon chairman, and building committee members.

Building Perimeters

Purchase baseline chalk (used for baseball diamond lines, available at hardware stores) and mark off the estimated outline of the building. Ask the crowd to stand around the building outline for a dedication prayer and for the shovel ceremony. The shovelers stand in the center and shovel dirt for a photograph.

Circle the Shovels

For an alternate idea, ask everyone attending the ceremony to gather around the shovelers for a time of prayer and dedication.

The Program

The groundbreaking ceremony should be held outdoors on the actual site of the proposed building. It should be celebratory, upbeat, and brief. Since this is an important event, it must be well planned. Make a minute-by-minute plan for those on the program. The highlight of the event will be a time of dedication prayer followed by a shovel ceremony, symbolically breaking the ground for the coming building.

Live Music

An important element of the groundbreaking celebration will be live music. Use upbeat Christian music that fits your church's worship style. Music should be playing as people arrive, creating a festive atmosphere. If possible, incorporate musical instruments and borrow or rent a sound system. As soon as the formal program is finished and people are dismissed to snack and fellowship, crank up the music once again. Since it's an outdoor event, consider creating a separate secondary stage for music.

Snap!

Recruit a church member with a good digital camera to take lots of photographs during the event. One great idea: consider using a nearby rooftop or a ladder to get an overview shot of the shovel ceremony and the group around the building parameters. Send the best photo to the local newspaper, associational newsletter, and church denominational state paper.

Ya Gotta Eat

It's a rule. There must be food. So when the groundbreaking ceremony program ends, dismiss the crowd to enjoy light refreshments. If you expect a huge crowd, set up multiple serving sites. You might want to serve "Groundbreaking Dirt Cake" using a window-box flower planter filled with pudding. Oreos are crumbled on top for the "dirt" along with artificial flowers to match your color scheme. The fellowship time will be high-spirited and enjoyable today!

Memento

Add excitement to your groundbreaking ceremony by planning ahead to distribute a memento to those who attend. Promotional items may be ordered by the gross and can be personalized for a reasonable cost. Ideas: magnet, pen, paperweight, key chain. You could even order clear glass or plastic vials, fill them with dirt from the site, and engrave or print a theme Scripture, along with the church name and event title.

Join Us!

Each person who attends the groundbreaking should receive a personal invitation to join your church in reaching the community for Christ. Invite them to register to receive regular e-mail updates. Invite them to worship with you next Sunday. Invite them to pray for your church during the building project.

Balloon Release

I've attended groundbreaking events where they organized a balloon release at the end of the ceremony. Print an invitation to worship on Sunday on small notes and place them inside the balloons. You never know where it might land. You could, instead, provide confetti shooters for children to use at the appropriate time.

Guests in Worship

There's a stranger in our worship service.

"I was a stranger and you took Me in."

—Matthew 25:35

Some dos and don'ts for making guests welcome during the worship service.

Secret Codes

"You're invited to AOV in the MAC after WMU." How rude can we be? *Never* use acronyms in your Sunday bulletin or verbal announcements! Decode your church lingo so guests can understand what's going on. Here's a fun cure: Just between staff members and leaders who speak from the podium on Sundays, levy a penalty of a quarter for every time they use an acronym without explaining it. A collection jar in the church office can collect the change, and it can be donated to the greeter fund.

Membership Card

Some churches place a church membership card in every church pew, along with offering envelopes. During the invitation people are invited to bring the membership card to the front to inquire about joining.

Climb Right In

Don't make guests climb over you to be seated. Happily move down. Better yet, leave some aisle seats open. Don't reserve seats and make it difficult for newcomers to find somewhere to sit. Never ever, say to a guest, "Hey! That's my pew!"

Fellowship Registry

Some churches place a clipboard or folder at the end of every pew. At the appropriate time during worship, the clipboard is passed down the aisle as each person, both church member and guest, completes the simple registration form. A lined chart on the clipboard has blanks for name, address, telephone, and e-mail address. Guests check "1–2" or "3 or more" to indicate how many times a guest has visited. Another blank asks if they wish to join the church. There are boxes to check single or married, and age range choices. The last blank is for comments or prayer requests.

Guest Cards

Many churches invite guests to complete guest cards, which are found in the pew racks or tear-off cards in the bulletin. Some ask both members and guests to register attendance by placing the form in the offering plate.

Informal Handshakes

Many churches have a brief informal greeting time during the worship service, shaking hands and meeting one another. Be sure your church members make a big priority of personally welcoming *guests* during this time. Will someone offer friendship? Will someone invite guests to lunch? Will someone remember each guest's name?

Roundabout

I've attended several churches where members actually walked informally around the entire worship center, physically shaking hands with almost every member and guest.

Members Stand

As church members stand, guests are asked to remain seated until they receive a visitor's packet.

Want to Go with Me?

Members should boldly and joyfully invite guests to an upcoming event, a Bible class, or the guest reception to meet the pastor. Tell a teen about the upcoming youth camp. Invite a child to the kids' choir. Mention an upcoming concert or churchwide event. "Come and go with me" is kinder than "Just go to room 256."

Best Seat in the House

How does it look to a guest when the front section is almost empty? I've observed that in most growing churches, the front seats in worship are greatly desired. People vie for the best seat, eager and expectant about Sunday worship. In one church where we served, all the young adults crowded the front section of chairs. In another, the youth took the "front and center" area. If front pews are sparsely filled, meet with the Bible study group who is most enthusiastic about the Lord, and ask if they will faithfully sit at the front.

Get Your DVD

Guests are welcomed from the pulpit and invited to stop by after worship at the greeter table outside the worship center to pick up a DVD about the church.

Gift Bag

Guests are welcomed from the pulpit and requested to raise their hand so ushers can bring them a gift bag or an information folder. Ushers must be quick to avoid embarrassing guests.

No Guest Sits Alone

Friendly church members should watch for guests and sit nearby to help them feel welcome. If teens in your church sit together at the front of the sanctuary, train the friendliest leaders to seek out and invite teen guests to join them.

Guest Reception

Guests are welcomed from the pulpit and invited to a brief pastor's reception following worship. Directions to the reception area should be well marked. Encourage church members who meet a guest to escort them to the reception and introduce them to the pastor. When guests came by our church's guest reception, we served light refreshments, introduced them to church staff members wearing name tags, and gave them printed information about the church and a coffee mug with the church logo. Bonus: church members could easily identify newcomers because they were carrying a coffee mug!

Look Around

You don't have a guest reception room at your church? Our church emptied an overstuffed storage closet just outside our church's worship center, added a large glass window and nice décor, and it made a very nice site. You might use a nice church office area or church parlor or library. Place a guest book at the entrance, and add a couple of chairs and a table for snacks. The key to your reception room, of course, is the warmth of the greeters.

Back-Row Baptist

This can actually be an assigned job! Every church needs a "back-row Baptist" who will watch for guests and ensure that not one leaves the building without a warm welcome and an invitation to lunch!

Counting Ceiling Tiles

Guests are carefully observing church members during worship. Remember that you're here to worship a living, loving God. This is no time to make a grocery list or take a quick nap. Don't look at your watch or act impatient. Sing. Worship. Take notes. Open your Bible. They'll be watching.

Sinners Welcome Here

Jesus died for sinners. So why would we roll our eyes or huff if one walks through our church doors? Don't be bothered by skin color, social status, or clothing of guests who come to your church. Show love to the pierced, the plaid, or the puny. Accept them with love; Jesus does.

The Invitation Shuffle

Avoid the Baptist dance called "the invitation shuffle." Guests around you may be considering eternity during the invitation, and if you begin banging your watch, gathering your belongings, or sneaking toward the exit, they may even miss heaven! Don't give guests the impression that your pot roast is more important than your God.

Cookies on the Doorknob

If your church is near a university campus, here's a great idea. A team delivers a bag of homemade cookies with a "Glad you came today" note to the dorm of first-time student visitors before they return to the dorm from church.

Top 10 Ways to Be Sure Guests Don't Come Back

10. Never ask a guest's name. If you somehow discover it, certainly don't call them by name. You don't want to get too friendly on the first visit.

9. Never sit near or beside a guest at church. If they look uncomfortable or lonely, don't worry. It's not your responsibility.

8. Look generally miserable. Frown often. Make it obvious that church is a serious thing and smiles are inappropriate.

7. Hallways should be empty when guests arrive. You mustn't overwhelm them, after all. Guests can discover their own route to worship or class.

6. Don't invite a guest to your Sunday school class or church events. You don't want to appear too forward. Never invite a guest to lunch with you!

5. Sit at the end of the pew, allowing guests to climb over you. Reserve seats for friends and hold your ground if a guest tries to infringe. If a guest is seated there when you arrive, firmly let him know it's your pew. Your comfort is more important than making it easy on unchurched guests.

4. Tell the guest how many years you have been a member of the church. Point out that many church members are related. That way he'll clearly understand that he will always be an outsider here.

3. Count the ceiling tiles during worship. Eat mints. Look at your watch often. Write a grocery list. Take a nap. Don't sing or open a Bible or take sermon notes. Whisper loudly to your kids and allow them to roam in and out of the service at their leisure.

2. Snort softly if a guest arrives late. Roll your eyes if his child wiggles. If a guest is dressed inappropriately, just shake your head. Generally ignore the guest if his skin color or social status does not match yours.

1. During the invitation, gather your personal belongings. Feel free to leave during the invitation, since you have important things waiting. If a guest is considering making a decision for Christ, he'll probably make it whether you're there or not.

Note: If your church truly wants to reach total strangers for Jesus Christ, consider doing the exact opposite of these ten instructions.

Homebound Ministry

Add a little zing to shut-in ministry.

"When did we see You sick, or in prison, and visit You?"

—Matthew 25:39

Need fresh idea to impact lives of homebound members?

Traveling Tea Party

Add a fun dimension to a homebound visit by taking a portable tea party with you. Fill a beautiful basket with china teacups and saucers, an attractive serving plate of scones or cookies, teapot, pretty napkins, specialty decaf tea bags or leaves and a strainer, and a thermos of boiling water. With great ceremony, place the napkin on the homebound friend's lap, pour tea, and serve cookies. Pray together, thanking God for a chance to celebrate one of His special children today. Even better: plan the tea party on her birthday or Valentine's Day.

Personal Delivery

Make a brief weekly delivery to a homebound member. Take a Sunday church bulletin, sermon tape, audio of a class Bible study, or a church library book.

Read the Word

If you visit the same homebound person every week, consider reading the Bible together. If you read for thirty minutes, you'll easily complete reading the entire New Testament in a year.

Lord's Supper

Deacons in our church went in twos or threes to administer the Lord's Supper to homebound members quarterly. They made an appointment and arrived dressed in suit and tie. The brief but reverent observance included Scripture reading, service of the elements, and prayer. Some teams would even sing favorite hymns.

Girls Only

A girls' or ladies' Sunday school class could "adopt" a female homebound church member for a year. Monthly visits could involve delivering a candlelit birthday cake, doing a manicure for her, planting flower bulbs in her yard, raking her leaves, etc. Take a tape recorder on each visit, and ask her one short question. Be sure she shares her Christian testimony and stories of how God has worked in her life. Conclude each visit with a prayer, led by different girls in the class. At the end of the year, present her with the cumulative recording of the interviews with the girls' autographs on the CD.

Gift of Music

Our church choir delivered live music to each homebound member as part of their Christmas party. Choir members were divided into trios and quartets, and each group was assigned to visit and carol for two homebound members. It was a favorite choir tradition. Wouldn't it be meaningful if an ensemble group prepared several old-time gospel songs and sang a personal concert for each homebound member of the church sometime during the year?

Happy Day

What a joy you would share if you arrive at a homebound member's home on his or her birthday with a lighted birthday cake! Or drop by on Valentine's Day with candy or a card. Or take an Easter lily or poinsettia during important holidays.

Little Things

Before you leave, ask your homebound friends if they would like help with replacing a lightbulb or a smoke alarm battery. Often small tasks are difficult for homebound people.

Light Brigade

A team of women or men can plan one-hour work projects to assist homebound or invalid church members. Our Light Brigade had a list of projects they enjoyed, such as planting flowers, painting a door, or rearranging a pantry. Each job could be completed by the team in one hour.

Library

"Bring my books, and especially my papers."

—2 Timothy 4:13 (NLT)

Give the gift of discipleship and entertainment and education to your congregation. Need fresh ideas to highlight your church library?

The Place to Be

The best way to increase book usage is to increase traffic in your library. Carefully create an inviting atmosphere with fresh paint, shelving, and art. Add comfortable seating, such as an armchair and lamp, similar to popular bookstores. Play "elevator" Christian music. Encourage people of all ages to "hang out" by creating an atmosphere of acceptance and welcome.

You'll Love This New Book

List new library book titles monthly in the church newsletter.

Look Inside!

If your library area is dark and uninviting, consider cutting out sections of the wall near the entrance and adding large glass windows. The library will be brighter and more enticing to passersby.

Up the Wattage

By simply updating overhead lighting or using higher wattage, the entire library atmosphere could change.

Add Coffee?

It's an amazing phenomenon: coffee belongs in bookstores these days. Why not add a cappuccino machine, teapot, or coffee to your church library? It will help create a hang-out atmosphere, enticing more people to stop by.

We're Open

If you want a successful church library, it must be available when church members are coming and going to most church activities. Post regular hours, but attempt to open the library before and after most special events, too.

In and Out

Make the checkout process simple to use. A cumbersome checkout system discourages library use. Add a drop slot on or near the library door to ease book return procedures.

We Have a Library?

Location is important for a church library. But even an undesirable location can be partially overcome with great directional signs and consistent promotional visibility. Send a note to all Sunday school or church members to invite them to enjoy the church library. Invite preschool classes to stop by for a weekly story time. Stock an attractive rolling cart with your most current books and allow people in a different building to check out books easily. Deliver new books and tapes to the senior adult class.

What's That Smell?

If aged books give your library a moldy smell, consider storing those books in a different area. Feature the newest and most requested books near the entrance, and keep a posted list of newly acquired reading.

Read This

Many library users will enjoy recommended reading lists. If your pastor or other church leaders or library volunteers love reading, ask them to recommend books they enjoy, then create a "recommended reading section" of books. Print a card to display by each book, "Recommended by Bill Bozeman, deacon" with a two-sentence recommendation worded by Bill himself. A separate section for "top teen reading" could feature books recommended by the pastor and youth leaders for teens.

Sermon Section

The library may be an appropriate place to process requests for copies of your pastor's sermons. It is fast and inexpensive to make CDs or audiotapes immediately after each worship service.

Add a Computer

Add a new or donated computer for patrons. Install software for Bible research, such as Bible Navigator, and place a sign on it that asks, "Looking for something in the Bible? Check here." Place an icon to help users read the plan of salvation, research mission agencies supported by your church, read the church newsletter, and play missions videos.

Kids Story Time

Advertise a "free kid's story time" at 10:00 a.m. Mondays and Fridays during the summer. Distribute notes in the community, post flyers in the park, and advertise it in the local newspaper. A gifted storyteller in your church simply reads Christian children's books for half an hour while parents browse the library. Information about church services is given to guests.

Recommended Summer Reading

Select new and classic Christian novels, and discipleship and study books to create a list of vacation reading books for adults, teens, and children.

Summer Reading Program

Your church librarian may create a Christian summer reading program for adults or children with a point system and award certificates.

In Memory Of

Often church members and friends may want to purchase a library book instead of flowers in memory of someone. Keep a list of desired books and their prices, and invite them to choose a book from the list. Place a printed sticker in the front cover of the book acknowledging "Given in memory of. . . ." Print a listing in the church newsletter or bulletin of books donated in memory of friends and invite church members to check out the books from the library.

How to Get New Books

Always keep a current list of desired Christian books, along with a price list, for your church library. Users may inquire about contributing new books, and you'll be ready. Encourage members of your church who purchase Christian book to donate them to the library when they finish reading. Acknowledge books purchased in memory of friends, and others will follow suit. Strive to place a budget item, however small, in the overall church budget for new library books. If a Sunday school class is considering a substitute for exchanging gifts with one another, they might enjoy drawing names and purchasing a library book in that person's honor.

Climb Up There

If your library is spacious, build cushioned cubbies for children's reading areas. Add a kid-sized table and chairs and display books on children's eye level.

Lord's Supper

"Do this in remembrance of Me."

—1 Corinthians 11:24

Small enhancements can positively impact this holy ordinance. Need fresh ideas?

Rope Off Rear Seating

To enhance intimacy for a Lord's Supper service, use cords to rope off rear seating. Or for a real change, ushers reverently seat worshippers as they arrive, filling up the first pew completely, then the second pew, and so on.

Personal Invitation

During the week prior to the Lord's Supper observance, deacons in our church create anticipation by calling every church member to invite them personally.

Sing

While elements are being distributed, the music leader, seated at the front, reverently sings the first verse of familiar hymns about the cross, smoothly transitioning between hymns. The music leader casually indicates that the congregation should softly sing along.

Personalized

As a meaningful alternative, try this presentation of the Lord's Supper. The pastor invites the congregation to come reverently, a few at a time, to receive the Lord's Supper at one of several small cloth-covered tables spaced across the front of the sanctuary. A staff minister or deacon reverently serves at each table, simply distributing each element and saying "Do this in remembrance of him." Participants come as a family, with friends, or with people seated near them. An usher at the front of each aisle quietly directs groups to the next available table.

Individual Prayer

Vary the personalized method above by stationing a deacon in each aisle to pray with each group before they go forward to receive Communion, which is served by pastoral staff.

Around the Tables

Near Thanksgiving our church traditionally enjoyed a simple meal of soup and cornbread in our fellowship hall. A deacon or minister was seated at each table. To observe the Lord's Supper, lights were dimmed, leaving only candlelight centerpieces. The pastor led the service, directing the deacons to distribute the elements at their individual table at the appropriate time.

Music Extraordinaire

Set a special mood for every Lord's Supper service by providing live preservice music, using a unique instrument such as a harp, xylophone, or bagpipe. Feature music during the service by your church's best ensemble or soloist.

This Is Special

Communicate importance for the Lord's Supper by using beautiful linens, candlelight, or fresh flowers from a member's garden. Dim the lights. Consider a poignant dramatic skit, dramatic reading, or responsive Scripture reading.

What He Means to Me

It was a tradition in our church for a new deacon to share his personal testimony at each Lord's Supper service.

How about Sunday Morning?

If you normally observe the Lord's Supper on Sunday evenings, consider planning it occasionally during morning worship. The Lord's Supper is also appropriate for a Maundy Thursday service or a Christmas Eve candlelight service.

Who's on First?

The Lord's Supper is an important, reverent ordinance and must not reek of confusion. The distribution of elements should be well rehearsed to flow smoothly. Servers can plan their attire to show reverence and continuity. In one church that might mean they all wear dark long-sleeved shirts; in another it could mean suits or sport coats.

Unleavened or Loaf

A church member might prepare homemade unleavened bread for the Lord's Supper celebration. Unleavened bread in large cracker form is available at many groceries. You could use large round loaves of bread from a bakery, asking recipients to tear off a piece.

Pass the Elements

If you normally distribute bread and juice for the Lord's Supper separately, you can change the process slightly by using a special tray that holds both elements or by passing the bread tray then the juice tray right behind it.

Silent Service

For a meaningful "come and go" Lord's Supper service, present worshippers an instruction page and small candle as they arrive. Several tables of bread and juice are set up across the front of the dimly lit sanctuary, and soft music plays. A large lighted candle, representing Christ, sits in a square of decorated floral foam near the front. (If this is a Christmas Lord's Supper and you have observed Advent, use the Christ candle.) The instruction page charges each person to sit silently in a pew for a time of personal examination and prayer, to read the scriptural account of the Lord's Supper, and then go alone to a table to partake of the bread and juice. To symbolize a commitment to shine for him, each person lights his candle from the Christ candle and places it firmly in the display before leaving silently.

Lord's Supper Reenactment

For one special Lord's Supper, thirteen men wore costumes and silently reenacted the Lord's Supper during an appropriate solo. A low table was set on the stage, and lights were lowered. A Lord's Supper reenactment can make an effective Maundy Thursday service.

Exchange Cups

One Lord's Supper our pastor preached on Christian forgiveness and fellowship. After distributing the cup, he asked congregation members to go silently to a person who has ministered to them, to someone who has been a great Christian example, or to anyone they need to offer or ask forgiveness and wordlessly exchange cups with them before the congregation drank the cup. As worshipful music played, this reverent movement and meaningful symbolism was effective.

Members in Service

"*The harvest is abundant, but the workers are few.
Therefore, pray to the Lord of the harvest to send out
workers into His harvest.*"

—Luke 10:2

They didn't move away or leave or die. So why do we sometimes ignore those from our class who are teaching in Sunday school? Consider these fresh ideas.

Wall of Honor

Use one wall of your classroom to create an attractive display to recognize your class's members in service, those members who fit the age division of your class but teach in a different preschool, children, youth, or adult Bible class on Sunday mornings. Feature a flattering photo of each member and the name of the class he or she teaches. Leave room in the display for additional teachers God may call out from your class.

Show and Tell

Take five minutes of class time annually to spotlight a member in service. Invite them to tell the class about the class they teach, either in person or by preparing a brief video. If they teach children, they might bring their class to your room to share a Scripture they've learned and allow your class to pray for them.

Lend a Hand

Offer to assist your class's members in service with occasional special projects. For example, if they teach youth, prepare a huge bag of snacks for their class to enjoy at youth camp. If they teach a Spanish Bible class, purchase Spanish Bibles for newcomers. If they teach toddlers, purchase a needed toy. Plan a joint class fellowship. Offer to substitute teach for them. Creatively encourage your members in service.

Fellowship Invitation

Include your members in service on class phone lists, class newsletters, and e-mail lists. Members in service should receive both a verbal and a written invitation to every class fellowship. Let them know how important they are by delivering a fancy invitation right to their classroom. When they attend a fellowship, introduce them to newcomers and share about God's blessings on their ministry.

Prayer

Remember to pray for your class's members in service each Sunday. Thank God for their faithfulness and ask his blessings on the class they teach.

We Prayed for You Today

Occasionally send a note, signed by all the class, to remind members in service of your prayers for them.

Midweek Services

> Worthwhile
> Wednesdays.

> *"And every day they devoted themselves to meeting
> together in the temple complex."*
>
> —Acts 2:46

Small things can make big impact on midweek gatherings at church. Need some fresh ideas?

Logo Aprons for Servers

If your church has Wednesday evening fellowship dinner, purchase inexpensive bib aprons by the dozen and monogram the church logo or motto on them.

Sign Holders

Purchase plastic 4 x 6 sign holders at a restaurant supply store for each dining table. Display Wednesday evening schedules and room numbers for all ages on one side and upcoming church events on the other side.

Deacon Servers

At our church, our deacons served Wednesday dinners (Acts 6:2–3). Using a rotation schedule, they demonstrated joyful fellowship and servant leadership. Aprons were personalized with their names. Our deacons' fellowship was strengthened, and members were quickly able to know and recognize them.

Pastor's Table

Give a printed invitation to new members of your church for a free Wednesday dinner with the pastor at a special pastor's table. If there are extra seats at the table, invite their Bible study teacher or another church member their age to join them. Treat them like royalty! Make a "Welcome New Members" table sign and print their names on place cards. Give them a small gift, such as a church license plate cover. At our church the deacons actually buss the pastor's table, and church members make a great effort to stop by to reintroduce themselves to new members. Best of all, the pastor can learn names, hear stories of the new members' Christian walk, discover interests and gifts, and help them plug into ministry and friendships.

Interlopers Welcome

Occasionally advertise Wednesday dinners on your church's exterior sign, i.e. "Join us for dinner Wednesday at 6:00 p.m. Dirt Cheap Price. Invaluable Conversation!" Be sure friendly members are ready to assimilate guests.

Summer Schedule

Summertime Wednesday evening schedules might be more informal. For example, our church adjusted Wednesday menus to a lighter fare of salad, soup, and loaded baked potato. Our Wednesday evening prayer service was held around the dinner tables.

Family Rate

Aid families by limiting the maximum cost per family or offering reduced rate children's meals. If possible, provide meals free for church staff families.

Add Simple Extras

Don't get in a rut. Live or recorded background music is always a nice touch. Rearrange the dining tables. Add fresh flowers from a member's garden. Add a strolling violinist for one evening. Have youth servers for a change. Keep Wednesday evening meals fresh with occasional surprises.

Reservations

To help with planning dinners, request an RSVP by using a tear-off in Sunday's worship bulletin for one-time or standing reservations. Reservations can also be called in to the church office.

Pew Prayers

As part of your Wednesday prayer meeting, invite attenders to each stand by a pew in the sanctuary and pray that God will speak to every person who will sit there Sunday.

Prayer Teams

Here's a wonderful Wednesday evening prayer meeting idea! At Bridgeport Central Baptist Church in Indianapolis, Pastor Gary Mullinex assigns Wednesday attenders to one of seven prayer teams. Each team has a different assigned prayer topic, but the topics rotate weekly so every team will pray for all topics during a seven-week period.

Team 1: The Lost. Pray for specific requests, the lost in our community, and Sunday guests.

Team 2: Church Families. Pray by name, using a church membership list.

Team 3: Physical Needs. Uses hospital list and prayer list.

Team 4: Praises. God loves to hear these!

Team 5: Government. Pray from a list of local and national leaders,

Team 6: Services/Leaders. Pray for Sunday and for each church leader on a list.

Team 7: Opportunities. Pray for new opportunities for the church.

Attenders remain on the same team each week and pray for different topics each week. Newcomers are assigned to a team as they attend.

Military Support

Remind that soldier
of God's love
and care.

"Don't worry about anything."

—Philippians 4:6a

A church family becomes important when soldiers are serving in a foreign country. Need fresh ideas to encourage them?

We're Praying for You

Especially during war times, create a prayer bulletin board at the church, featuring photos and mailing addresses of all church members serving in the military. You could include relatives and friends of members as well. Mail a snapshot of the bulletin board to each soldier featured.

Witnessing Sour Patch Kids

When our singles Sunday school class sent a big package of Sour Patch Kids candies to a church member stationed in Iraq, he said it opened more witnessing opportunities than he'd ever had!

Greeting Cards

Wouldn't it be fun for a soldier to receive a card from every member of the class or church mailed separately? Choose a holiday or birthday, distribute the soldier's address, and challenge the group to minister to that soldier. Better yet, distribute cards, allowing each member to write personalized notes and encouragements, then collect them and mail one daily.

What to Write

Your church or Bible class is writing to a person in the military, but you're not personally acquainted. Don't know what to write? How about a verse of Scripture, a personal note from the pastor, a photo of your church's bulletin board for military prayer, the church newsletter or bulletin, notes and art from a children's Sunday school class, local newspaper articles. If it's a group project, include a group photo with a stick-on word bubble declaring, "We're praying for you!"

Holiday Packages

A Bible class, deacon team, choir, youth group, or individual church member can impact a soldier's holiday by sending a personalized package. Ideas to include: a tiny Christmas tree, a children's book of the Christmas story, a Christmas ornament, little homey things to make holidays seem more like holidays. Hard candies, energizer bars, gum, sunflower seeds, trail mix, cookies, gum, pop tarts. Christian CD or DVD, paperback book, travel-size board game, bookmark, toothpicks, tracts, sundries, phone calling card, disposable camera. Most importantly, include a note reminding the soldier of God's love and your church's consistent prayers. Then as you seal the parcel, pray for that soldier.

Minister Ordination

*"It is a true saying that if a man wants to be a pastor
he has a good ambition."*

—1 Timothy 3:1 (TLB)

What a privilege for a church to ordain one of its own to Christian ministry.
Need fresh ideas for the service?

Ordination Certificate

Ask each ordained minister and deacon who attends the service to sign the
back of the ordination certificate.

Hear His Story

As part of the minister's ordination service, invite him to share about his call
to ministry.

Ministry Mentor

If the new minister has a mentor or a family member in the ministry, invite that
pastor to participate in the service.

Ordination Invitations

Print formal invitations to the minister's ordination service and mail them to
his friends and relatives and local pastors.

Ordination Gift

For a nice ordination gift, present the newly ordained minister with a leather
Bible signed by all ordained deacons and ministers present.

Reception

Plan a fellowship reception in the new minister's honor after the formal ceremony.

A (Lego) Wall of Prayer

When Paul Hollis, a member at Oakhills Baptist in Evansville, Indiana, was ordained to the ministry, those who attended were given a Lego building block as they arrived. They wrote their name in permanent pen on the side. The service ended with an invitation for each guest to commit to pray for Paul and his ministry. Those attending the ceremony affirmed their commitment by coming to the front prayerfully and silently presenting him their building block. Brother Hollis built a small wall from the blocks, and he keeps it on his desk to remind him of the wall of prayers surrounding his ministry.

Minister's Anniversary

"Now we ask you, brothers, to give recognition to those who labor among you and lead you in the Lord and admonish you, and to esteem them very highly in love because of their work."

—1 Thessalonians 5:12–13

Ever notice that growing churches have long-term pastors? Celebrate yours with these fresh ideas.

Say the Words

Every year on your minister's anniversary, print a congratulations and thank-you note in the Sunday bulletin and make an announcement during Sunday morning worship to say "thank you" for his ministry in your church. A boutonniere for the pastor and flowers for his wife would be appropriate. If it's a five-year or five-year-increment anniversary, plan a big celebration (examples below) to honor God and his workman.

Balloon Prayers

Present a balloon prayer bouquet. Get one balloon for each year of ministry (i.e. ten years = ten balloons). Ask church members to commit to pray and fast for God's blessings and wisdom for your pastor on one of the next ten days. Place names of the people who are praying on that day inside each balloon, allowing the pastor to discover daily who is praying.

Anniversary Reception

Whether the anniversary reception is formal or informal, make it personal. Ask each church member to bring a personal letter to the pastor on an 8½ x 11 piece of paper, then place them in a memory book. Take a photo of the minister with each person who attends, and place those photographs in the book with their letter.

Thirty Surprises for Thirty Years

If your pastor is celebrating a large anniversary, such as the thirtieth, recruit thirty faithful church members for a special surprise. At the end of the celebration party, inform the pastor that for the next thirty days, the celebration will continue with one surprise each day.

Celebration Banquet

Invite the whole church. Serve the pastor's favorite food. Ask everyone to wear his favorite color, and use that color for décor. Invite his favorite friends and relatives from other cities and help pay their way to attend. Ask the entire group to quote his favorite Scripture together. Present his wife a bouquet of her favorite flowers. Prepare an autograph book of notes from church members with each person signing his or her name and "your favorite church member" beneath.

Roast Pastor

Plan a "roast," assuring that it's encouraging and flattering. Videotape the comments for the pastor to enjoy again and again.

Paul E. Miller Day

When celebrating a lengthy pastoral anniversary, such as a twenty-fifth, talk with city officials about declaring a one-time "Pastor Paul E. Miller Day" in your city (substituting your pastor's name, of course). They will issue an official document, and the mayor may even show up to present the proclamation!

Very Special

If a minister at your church is celebrating a decade (tenth, twentieth, etc.) anniversary, make it extra special. Our church sent a staff member who loved tennis on an all-expense-paid trip to the Wimbledon in England. We bought a small car for our hospital minister when she celebrated twenty years. One pastor was presented one thousand dollars for each year he had served as pastor. Another church planned a "this is your life" type party. Surprise guests were backlit as they stood behind a screen and told stories about the pastor. You could plan a "world's best shepherd" party, with a sheep theme. Make it fit your community and your beloved pastor, and celebrate longevity in the ministry.

Ministering to the Sick

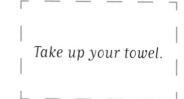

Take up your towel.

"I was sick and you took care of Me."

—Matthew 25:36

It's Christianity in action. Need fresh ideas for ministering to the ill?

Progressive Floral Arrangement

Here's a meaningful class or church project for a sick person. One person from your church or Bible class delivers a vase containing just a few flowers. Once daily for the next several days, different visitors from your group drop by to deliver a few more fresh flowers from their garden or florist, gradually creating a massive bouquet.

Puzzle Photo

For a long-term illness, take a group photo of your Bible class and send it to an online puzzle company to create a thousand piece jigsaw puzzle. They can add word bubbles above a few people, such as "Get well," "We're praying for you," "I miss you most!" or, "If you don't get well soon, we're having Sunday school at your house!"

Pillowcase

For a thoughtful gift during an extended hospital stay, members of your class or church can sign their names in permanent marker on a bright yellow pillowcase, adding art, Scripture, encouraging words and funny notes.

Prayer Pager

For a long-term or critical illness, get a pager for the patient. Distribute the pager telephone number to all church members and friends of the patient, asking them to pray for the patient, dial the pager number, enter their zip code and the # key, then e-mail another Christian to ask them to do the same. Give the patient a listing of zip codes across the country to check off zip codes where people are praying for him or her.

Guest Book

Be the first visitor at the hospital, and bring along a guest book for the sickroom.

Collective Gift Basket

Prepare a lovely basket from your group, asking members to bring a favorite video movie or audiobook, labeled with their name, for a long-term loan. When your friend is well, he can return the collection in class.

Curb Loneliness

Once the patient is feeling better but still housebound, ask if you can bring home-cooked, store-bought, or picnic dinner and leisurely dine together.

One-a-Day Treats

Distribute a note card to members of your group, asking them to write a personal note of encouragement to the patient. Collect the notes, and mail one each day. Or prepare a basket of small, carefully selected, wrapped gifts, and ask the patient to open one each day.

Scripture Delivery

It's a perfect gift for a hospital visit. Take a Scripture! Write the words from a comforting Scripture and give it to the patient.

Text Message Prayer Reminder

If the patient has a cell phone, friends can text message him or her often to remind them they're praying.

Take This

Deliver a church bulletin along with a recording of last Sunday's sermon and Sunday school Bible study. You could include a recording of the Bible study group singing a funny song for the patient.

If the Cast Fits

If the patient has mobility problems, use permanent markers to sign your name, write notes and Scriptures, or draw art on an inexpensive cane.

Wisdom Drinks

For a wisdom tooth removal patient, schedule different class members to arrive every four hours for two days delivering Jell-O, a milkshake, a slurpee, broth, or a soft drink.

I Feel Your Pain

Some men in the young adult Sunday school class shaved their heads to match a chemo patient's and delivered a group photo when they arrived to visit.

Emergency Room Basket

Ladies at our church obtained permission from the local hospital to prepare a snack basket to place in the emergency room. They purchase a large basket, decorate it, and hang a laminated note, "First Baptist Church is praying for you today. Call 222-2222 to request specific prayer." The women's ministry and ladies' Sunday school class regularly collect wrapped snack items to replenish the basket, and seven ladies were assigned a specific day to stop by the hospital and fill the snack basket. Our church prayer chapel often receives calls with prayer requests, and many times the ladies get to pray with people they met.

Missionary Encouragement

"Finally, pray for us, brothers, that the Lord's message may spread rapidly and be honored."

—2 Thessalonians 3:1

They're busy about his business every day. They're away from home. And they need your encouragement. Need fresh ideas?

Autographs

Help children in your church to value missionary speakers by encouraging them to get their autograph.

Live Update

Choose a missionary from those supported by your church—and work out logistics for a live audio phone chat or video feed during a worship service. Ask, "What's Jesus doing in Kiev, Ukraine (missionary's ministry area)?" A five-minute chat can give church members a personalized view of worldwide missions.

Got It

If you subscribe to a missionary's e-mail newsletter, reply when you receive it. Just a quick note, such as, "Got it. Prayers going up!" is an encouragement to them. Even better, offer a comment or compliment about some specific aspect of their ministry and a renewed commitment to pray for that missionary.

Someone Remembered

When a person is away from home, mail matters. Send a birthday card, holiday card, or Scripture card. Or send a personal encouragement note on the first day of every month.

Five-Year Plan

A children's class or missions group can "adopt" a missionary family. Carefully choose a missionary family supported by your church that includes children near the same age of your group. Send monthly prayer notes and occasional gifts of encouragement. Mail an annual group photo with members' signatures. Missionaries will enjoy seeing names with faces of kids who pray for them, and each year they'll see them grow physically too. By consistently encouraging the same missionary family, your group can establish a long-distance relationship and can pray for specific needs.

Personalize It

Adults or children could make no-sew bibbed aprons with autographed hand-prints along with this note: "We pray for you!" A women's group could use colorful permanent pens to sign their names along the hem of a tablecloth as a prayer promise for a missionary. Before a group from your church leaves for a mission trip, create a really long scroll-type card. Ask every member of your church or class to sign the scroll or write notes of encouragement to the missionary, and send it "special delivery" with your mission team.

On Their Turf

Nothing encourages missionaries and impacts a church's commitment to missions like a mission trip. Consider unique abilities of your church members, confer with the missionary, then plan a mission trip to assist with a specific project. Your denomination's state office or missionary agency can help select a country and a missionary. Mission trips can be effectively planned for small or large groups, adults, singles, families, senior adults, or youth.

One Organizer

If your missions support group plans to encourage one missionary or missionary family, select one member of the group to organize the efforts. Everyone in your group can write a personal letter of encouragement at the same time, and the organizer can collect them and mail one note every week or two for the entire year. He or she can make copies of the missionary's newsletters and notes, research needs, victories, and prayer requests from that missionary.

That Beautiful Face

No, you probably can't display a photograph of every missionary supported by your church. Southern Baptists support more than ten thousand worldwide! Perhaps you could choose a few missionaries to spotlight each year, hang their photo in the prayer chapel or church library, and send a photo of that wall to the missionary. Our church had a hallway where we displayed a photograph of each missionary who was from our church, including those whose parents were members of our church. A small, framed flag hung below each photo.

Video Greeting Card

Prepare a video Christmas or birthday card for a special missionary you support. Include your whole Bible class or church in the video with a group song, individual comments, and prayer for the missionaries.

Furloughing Missionaries

When missionaries come stateside for furlough, it's a great opportunity for your church to encourage them. Provide a car for their use. Babysit their children for an occasional date night or special event. Include them in holidays and everyday events with your church or your family. Listen. Laugh. Care.

Missionary Speaker

When missionaries come to your church to speak, do something special to welcome them. Present them flowers. Purchase an assortment of products that represent your city. For example, in Indiana we could present a Vera Bradley bag, a Colts football jersey, Indiana popcorn, and chocolates.

MK Speakers

Some missionary kids (MK) would enjoy talking about the mission field with children or teens at your church. It could be set up in an interview style, with kids asking preplanned questions of interest to other kids. They might teach a game, song, or a few words of the foreign language. Conclude with a special time of prayer led by children.

MK Gifts

If a guest missionary speaker has a child, invite children in the same age group to a big picnic in the missionary kid's (MK) honor. Purchase a new book for the appropriate age, and allow the children to write notes in the front cover.

A Mission House

It's worth the investment if your church is able to purchase a home for furloughing missionaries to use while in the U.S.

Missions Education

*"Let all the inhabitants of the world stand
in awe of Him."*

—Psalm 33:8b

The more your church knows about missions, the more they'll care. Need some fresh ideas?

"To the Ends of the Earth" Film Festival

This may be the best event ever! Plan a twelve-hour, come-and-go film festival at your church, featuring quality missions videos and video clips produced by the International Mission Board (IMB). Teens will love the music videos and adventure scenes. The Mr. Christopher series will thrill kids and adults. Everyone will giggle at the "Eloise" clips and cry with the disaster ministry films. And they'll learn about more than five thousand international missionaries supported by your church. Recruit volunteer technicians, hosts and hostesses, and order the filmfest DVDs from the IMB (800-999-3113.) Show films back-to-back on a large screen, and serve popcorn and soft drinks. Print schedules so attenders can plan ahead. At exits, display church and missions brochures and collection boxes for missions offerings and ballots (below). If a missionary is furloughing nearby, invite him or her to introduce a few videos and to chat with viewers outside the screening area. As your church looks "to the ends of the earth," your whole church will be talking about missions!

Film Fest Winner

Add a fun element to your missions film fest by allowing each viewer to vote for their favorite video in several categories: shorts, clips, music video, and longs.

Everyone loves to give an opinion! Distribute ballots for every attender and provide a ballot box for collection. Announce the winning films during Sunday morning worship, and offer a final screening of the winning film.

Missions Room

Wouldn't it be wonderful to have a special room or an area of the church library specifically designed to educate about missions? A television could play looped versions of the quality missions videos provided by our mission agencies. A prayer corner could have a kneeling bench. Posters from your missions agencies could decorate the walls along with a world map showing missionary locations. Set up a computer with instructions for viewing your church mission Web sites. A telephone can be set up with the telephone number for missionary prayer requests and updates from your missions agencies. Provide cards and stationary to write notes to missionaries. Display a clock that shows times in various countries or mount multiple clocks on the wall set to different time zones. Display missions agency updates and missionary newsletters. Post a summary of local and international missions supported by your church.

Live Missionary

Nothing brings missions to life like a guest missionary speaker at your church. Contact your missions agencies or denominational office to arrange for a furloughing missionary to speak at your church.

Ukranians Welcome

If your missionary speaker serves in a foreign country, advertise in the local newspaper to invite people with ties to that country to attend the program and stay for a special reception with the missionary.

Free Borscht

Plan a reception after the missionary speaks and serve a unique dish from the country where your missionary speaker works. Church members will enjoy an informal opportunity to ask questions and visit with the missionary.

Missions Month

Our church emphasized missions for one entire month each year. In every worship service that month, we promote missions in some way. Each week highlights a different area of missions: international missions (International Mission Board), home missions (North American Mission Board), state missions, associational missions, and our local missions projects. Every service is extra special, and our church can't wait for missions month. Guest missionaries share testimonies or sermons. We have a huge missions fair. Instead of taking multiple offerings during the year, we collected one large offering to divide between our denomination's special missions offering. Our church's missions giving skyrocketed!

Virtual Bus Tour

Fall Creek Baptist in Indianapolis plans a virtual bus tour to promote North American Missions. Travel "tickets" are distributed to promote the event. For the Sunday evening service, chairs are arranged to look like buses with wheels and low paper walls. Each bus has a driver and tour guide. As they tour, passengers view video clips about North American Mission Board missionaries. Lively, creative tour guides distribute snacks and direct activities. For example, cheese is served as the bus "drives" through Wisconsin. The group participates in activities which relate to the destinations. They may pack a box for the seaman center or make salvation bracelets for a missionary in Rhode Island.

Missions Fair

┌ ─ ─ ─ ─ ─ ─ ┐
│ *Start a new missions* │
│ *tradition.* │
└ ─ ─ ─ ─ ─ ─ ┘

*"You will be My witnesses in Jerusalem, in all Judea
and Samaria, and to the ends of the earth."*

—Acts 1:8

It's an educational seminar. It's a party. No, it's a missions fair! Need fresh ideas
for planning one?

Acts 1:8 Illustrated

An annual missions fair is an effective way to educate and excite church members about all the ways your church is involved in missions. Plan a first-class
event with visual appeal, fast-paced schedule, themed food and music, and
entertaining exhibits to represent every facet of missions for your church.
Though each year's missions fair has a totally different theme and ambiance,
every missions fair will produce the same result: church members who are well
informed and inspired to support and participate in missions.

Showcase

Your church missions fair will feature dozens of exhibits—one to represent
every area of missions in which your church participates. Make a long list of
every local missions venture of your church. Are you planting a new church?
Do you have a clothes closet or food pantry for benevolent needs? Do you have
nursing home ministries? Planning a mission trip? List children's and adult
missions support groups. Next, consider missions-related associations of your
church, such as a local association of churches or your association's state convention. Add displays for missionaries supported by your church, both nationally and internationally. Enhance the fair by inviting local, state, national, and
international missionaries to attend.

Interactive and Educational

Each exhibit needs an interactive element. One year's missions fair may have a punch card with blanks for exhibitors to hole-punch. Another fair may have interactive games, hands-on projects, food samplings, scavenger hunt clues or interviews. Each exhibitor's goal is to draw in each person and excite and inform them about that missions opportunity. Though it's a party atmosphere, church members will be amazed to learn about all the missions projects and missionaries your church supports.

Missions Fair Themes

A missions fair team chooses a unique theme and prepares all year long for an unforgettable event. After decades of missions fairs at our church, not one fair looked alike! It's a highlight of the year for people of all ages, connecting them personally with missions. Some theme examples are given below.

Missions Fair Theme: My Missions Dollar

Design a missions "dollar bill" to give to guests. As guests view each missions exhibit, the appropriate portion is cut off his dollar.

Missions Fair Theme: The Tomorrow Show

All exhibits are designed as sets for missions talk shows with ongoing live interviews, scripted teen interviewers, video cameras, and lots of lights. Attenders stroll from set to set observing and learning.

Missions Fair Theme: Fly to Missions

This airport theme has a concourse area, tickets, music, food, and entertainment. Exhibits are set around the perimeter, with rows of chairs to simulate an airplane. Flight attendants take tickets and serve snacks as guests view short in-flight videos about each exhibit.

Missions Fair Theme: Mission Museum Classic

Tuxedoed docents give scripted tours through museum-style exhibits. Use art, collections, live mannequins, and classical music, of course! The use of light and space sets the mood. Trophy cases, pedestals, and easels can display items representing each missions effort. Play a missions videotape in a seated area.

Missions Fair Theme: The Greatest Glow on Earth

Create a big-top circus atmosphere, complete with a band, a tent, and a ringmaster. Each ministry area creates a "show" to demonstrate their mission, such as a ground-level tightrope, strong man, juggler, clowns, stilts, costumes, or balloons. Serve cotton candy and peanuts, of course.

Missions Fair Theme: Acts 1:8 Illustrated

Guests progress through several display areas representing your church's Jerusalem (missions in your city), Judea (in your state), Samaria (North American missions), and the uttermost parts of the world (international missions). A theme song can be interpreted uniquely in each area, i.e., oriental, country-western band.

Missions Fair Theme: Missions Safari

Rows of chairs, simulating a tour bus, are surrounded by plants and stuffed monkeys for a jungle theme. An enthusiastic tour guide narrates crocodile-hunter style as he bounces and "drives" the group on a missions tour. The exhibitors actually walk past the buses. For example, a passing group can sing in Spanish while the tour guide explains the Mexico missions trip.

Missions Fair Theme: Numbers Missions Fair

Huge glittered numbers at each exhibit represent an aspect of that ministry. For example, a 35 at the mission church exhibit denotes their number of members. Exhibits use number-related games, i.e., a jar of 5,370 jelly beans to challenge people to guess how many overseas missionaries you support.

Missions Fair Theme: Techno-Missions

Use modern décor and lighting. Feature high-tech displays using computers, audiovisuals, headphones, etc.

Missions Fair Theme: Drive-In Missions Fair

Create a minute-long looped video for each ministry area. A child with a toy steering wheel drives small groups from room to room to see the drive-in theater about those ministries. Serve movie snacks. Theater "personnel" can use flashlights to direct groups in and out.

Missions Fair Theme: A Missions Fair

Exhibits illustrate their missions project using carnival games—ball tosses, cakewalk, face paint, etc. Use carnival prizes and tickets for booths. Create a carousel with streamers and stick horses for children to "ride."

Missions Fair Theme: Time for Missions

Clocks are everywhere. Ring chimes every three minutes to move attendees from exhibit to exhibit. Each exhibit can use a clock theme for their interactive demonstration.

Missions Fair Theme: Missions in Fashion

The exhibits are glitzy, but the main event is a fast-paced missions fashion show. An enthusiastic announcer describes missions while creatively costumed "models" walk the runway. Example: An "inmate" carries prison bars and a Bible to represent prison ministry. Models in ethnic costumes represent foreign missions.

Missions Fair Theme: Light Your World

Exhibits use an assortment of lights. Overhead lights are dim, with a footprint pathway leading to each uniquely lighted exhibit.

Missions Fair Theme: Where's Monty Missionary?

The entire fair is a search for Monty, the missionary, through the exhibits. A full-length mirror for one exhibit with the title: "Go ye . . . YOU'RE a missionary!" to challenge every church member to tell others about Christ.

Missions Giving

"Therefore, we ought to support such men, so that we
can be co-workers with the truth."

—3 John 3:8

It's an investment in eternity. Need fresh ideas for missions giving?

The Face of Missions

Create two large visuals. Label one "challenge" and the other "victory." Obtain a small photo of every missionary your church supports, and use rubber cement to display them on the challenge board. Divide your church's goal for the missions offering by the number of missionaries. For example, if your church supports Southern Baptist's International Mission Board missionaries, you'll have 5,050 photographs. Try to set your mission offering in multiples of that number. For example, if you set your church goal for the offering at $5,050, that's one dollar per missionary. If the goal is $2,025, it's fifty cents per missionary. If it's $50,500, that's ten dollars per missionary. Each week, calculate dollars given toward the missions offering, then move the appropriate number of missionary photos to the victory board. If some members want to request a specific missionary photo, no problem. (For IMB photos, e-mail www.photo services.imb.org.)

Get Visual

For a visual reminder of a church annual giving goal for missions, place a large display of flags along the rear of the worship center. As each $100 (or appropriate increment) is given toward the goal, move one flag to the stage area. When all flags are transferred, the goal has been met. For example, one flag could represent $10 or $1000. For national missions offering, use state flags. For international missions, use international flags.

Missions Month

Our church took an entire month each year to celebrate missions and gather all of our mission offerings. It was well planned and greatly anticipated. Each week emphasized one specific area of missions—international, North American, state, associational and local missions. Some weeks featured a furloughing missionary to share a "Missions Moment" testimony or sometimes preach the sermon. We had missions exhibits, film clips, and live video feeds from the mission field. Each week was greatly anticipated. For example, on foreign mission emphasis Sunday, we may have a flag procession or greeters dressed in foreign costumes. The total missions offering was divided, using a percentage plan, between Lottie Moon international missions, Annie Armstrong North American missions, state missions offering, and associational mission offerings. Our church's giving to missions was larger than ever, and church members became enthusiastically informed about missions.

Lottie Moon Post Office

It's an old idea, but it still works. Many churches create a Lottie Moon Post Office, encouraging church members to send Christmas cards to other church members through the "post office." A donation of twenty-five cents per card is suggested, and the money goes to the Lottie Moon Christmas Offering for International Missions.

Missions Offerings

Some churches have contests (i.e. men vs. women) for bringing the most coins for a mission offering. Some have a "walk to the manger," where members are invited to bring their Lottie Moon offering to a manger display at the front of the worship area. I've seen churches do auctions, hold competitions between Sunday school classes, and host craft fairs.

Give and Gobble

Some ideas related to food and missions:
- Serve Lottie Soup and Mission Pie for a special missions donation (Keck Avenue Baptist, Evansville, Indiana). Or use her recipe on www.imb.org and serve Lottie Moon cookies.
- Lottie Moon Bake Shop receives large missions donations for homemade Christmas goodies (Oakhills Baptist, Evansville, Indiana).

- Annual Ham and Bean Dinner and auction for missions (Westside Baptist, Kokomo, Indiana).

Vacation Bible School Offering

Our church chose a specific missions project or designation for each year's Vacation Bible School offering. We built a huge scale, and children were challenged to bring money to outweigh our minister. Each day, he would climb up and sit on one side of the scale, tell a short missions story, and challenge the kids to try to outweigh him with their gifts! Another VBS mission offering idea: try to fill a huge container with coins, allowing kids to bring them to the front and put them inside.

Penny Annie

Challenge church members to collect their pennies all year long to give to the Annie Armstrong Offering for North American Missions.

Something to Brag About

Tell the story! It's exciting for church members to know that they are supporting quality, effective missionaries around the world. Display numbers. Use posters provided by our mission agencies. Incorporate one or two slides in your weekly preservice audiovisual announcements to tell about missions.

Mission Trips

*"We immediately made efforts to set out for Macedonia,
concluding that God had called us to evangelize them."*

—Acts 16:10

Your church is partnering with a missionary to send some members for a mission trip. Get ready for a blessing!

Share the Blessing!

Is a group from your church planning a mission trip to Africa or Houston or somewhere else? Don't leave out the rest of the church! Invite your church's third graders, senior adult men's class, deacons, choir, or any other church group to help with a specific project for the trip. They could assemble witnessing bracelet kits or staple booklets or make small gifts for children in a poverty area.

Pray for One

Individual members, a Sunday school class, or another church organization could "adopt" one member of a mission trip team, committing to pray daily while they are on the mission trip. Purchase inexpensive plastic bracelets, write the name of one mission team member on each bracelet, and distribute them to members who will commit to pray daily during the trip. The bracelet will be a tangible prayer reminder.

Planning Meetings

A missionary once told me, "There is no such thing as an over-prepared mission team." Schedule regular meetings for the mission team for planning and prayer. Make specific assignments for ministries and preparations. For example, one team may prepare a drama presentation, and another may be in charge of a

Vacation Bible School class. Work closely with your missionary contact so your efforts will fit that missionary's strategy of ministry.

Shared Research

At the first mission trip planning meeting, assign each member a topic to research about the destination—weather, customs, religions, money exchange, schools, and families. They could research about the missionaries you will assist and about the evangelistic work being done in that country. Some may prepare handouts about their topic. At each subsequent planning meeting, ask one or two team members to bring their report to the group.

Flexibility

At the first planning meeting for your mission trip, distribute pipe cleaners or bendy toys to each person on your mission trip team. Ask them to describe the item. Let them know from the beginning that flexibility is a key ingredient to any successful mission trip. Attach the pipe cleaner to your planning notebooks. One of our mission teams even made "flexibility" T-shirts to wear at meetings!

Collect Stuff

As the mission team plans their trip, members of the church may be able to help collect specific items to help. For example, if the team is planning a women's conference in a foreign country, the church could prepare small gifts for each attendee. If they are planning children's ministries, they might collect candies for workers to distribute. If they are leading a Vacation Bible School, church members could help collect supplies or prizes.

Tiny Photo Album

Each member of the team may prepare a small photo book of family, pets, church, job, and interests. The book can be helpful in sharing cultures and getting to know people in another country.

What a Team

You may consider asking the mission team to wear the same color shirts when you travel. Or order matching shirts to wear on a travel day. Or baseball caps or bandannas or scarves. Our senior adult mission team wore matching vests they'd made. You'll cause lots of interest, and you'll be less likely to lose one another.

Instruction Card

Prepare a small printed card for each mission team member with these details: name, address, and telephone number for the missionary, church, hotel, and embassy. The other side of the card could have some phrases of the language or a money exchange rate chart.

Share in the Air

For overseas travel or long flights, consider booking seat assignments in pairs rather than sitting in one large group. Pray with the entire group before departure, asking God to allow each person to share about him with their seatmate en route to your destination.

Less Is Less

Be specific with packing instructions for mission team members. A good rule of thumb for overseas travel: pack frugally, then remove at least half of what you packed. With careful planning most trips could limit luggage to one medium-sized bag, leaving the additional checked bag for supplies needed for the trip.

Carry Your Own

An important up-front, strictly enforced rule for any mission trip: You bring it; you carry it. Each mission trip team member carries and loads his or her own bags.

Wear 'em and Leave 'em

If your mission trip destination is a poverty area, ask the missionary there if it would be appropriate for your mission team to leave some of the clothes you wear during the trip. Most of us could spare a few articles of clothing. Just think, you'll bless someone, and you'll have space in your bag for souvenirs!

Cinch Sack

Ask youth going on foreign mission trips to take a cinch sack for their carry-on. It's an inexpensive cloth bag with string shoulder straps, available at sports stores. A cinch sack is lightweight and holds lots of stuff, a great invention for travel.

The Bags with the Yellow Ribbon

Purchase plenty of wide, brightly colored ribbon. Tie a small length of it on the handle of each bag of your mission team. When the team arrives at airport or hotel baggage pickup, the process will be greatly simplified.

Early Departure?

If your mission team has an early morning departure time and is traveling by bus or van, ask mission trip participants to bring luggage to the church the evening beforehand. Have a special time of prayer together, and pack baggage. The next morning will be much more relaxed.

A Cheer for Beef Jerky

Most overseas mission trips are planned to assist a missionary in the foreign country. Ask that missionary what small items you could bring to remind them of home. In one area of the world, they may not be able to get peanut butter, and another may not have dressing mix. When I told one missionary I wanted to bring something from the States, he enthusiastically requested some smoked jerky and a map he couldn't find in his country. Properly researched, a small gift makes an important impact. A group from your church may enjoy preparing a nice care package for you to deliver to the missionary.

Films and Magazines and Newspapers

Take magazines, current books, and a newspaper to missionaries serving where English isn't spoken. Missionary families with children may appreciate DVDs of good television shows and movies appropriate for their families.

Special Delivery

The foreign missionary where you're traveling for your mission trip may have difficulty receiving supplies or personal items, such as homeschool materials, personal interest items, or books. Let them know ahead of time that if they'd like to order something mailed to your home, you'll be glad to deliver it in person.

Thanks for the Bed

If you're staying in the home of a church member or missionary at your mission trip destination, take a nice gift to express thanks. Some suggestions: unique products or crafts from your home state.

Don't Forget the MK

If the missionary has children (MKs), wouldn't it be nice to take a special gift for them? A missionary's daughter loved drawing, so our team chipped in and took her a personalized wooden box of art supplies. She was delighted! And since she had to share her room with us during the trip, she definitely deserved a nice gift.

Daily Web Update

Take a digital camera and download photos of the mission trip daily so friends at home can experience missions with your team. The adult and children's mission groups, as well as parents and friends, will enjoy sharing the journey. When we were on a mission trip to Kiev, Ukraine, International Mission Board missionary Mary Ellen Ragains took daily photos and posted them on their missionary Web site. Everyone at home loved it. Current photos lend comfort to loved ones back home and encourage them to pray for the team. (Check out www.kievkonnect.com.)

Live Feed from India

Techies in your church can help arrange a brief live interview with your mission team during Sunday worship. When Pastor Patrick Hunter, Beacon Baptist Church, Shelbyville, Indiana, took a mission team to Mexico, they set up a live audio chat for a couple of minutes during the morning worship service. The pastor actually welcomed guests to worship and briefly shared about how God was working on in their trip. (No fancy equipment? Just hold a micophone to a speaker phone.) A live video would be even more effective. A one- or two-minute conversation can give the entire congregation a delightful taste of missions involvement.

Welcome Home!

A mission trip is hard work. Wouldn't it be fun for friends or parents who are picking up the team at the church or the airport to hold a "Welcome Home" banner, balloons, or flowers?

Sharing Photos

Collect digital photographs from all mission team members, compile them on one DVD, and make copies for all team members. If you use standard photos, ask team members to make double prints and share the extras at the debrief party.

Mission Team Debrief Party

Plan a gathering for your team shortly after returning from the mission trip to debrief and share photos. Retell stories and celebrate God's blessings during the mission trip. Invite family members and others who encouraged your team. Conclude with prayer for the missionaries where your mission team served and for God's continued blessings on their ministry. Then start planning next year's mission trip.

Mother's Day

Rise up and call her "blessed" today.

"She is far more precious than jewels."

—Proverbs 31:10

Need fresh ideas to honor moms?

Preschool Prayer Parade

Teach an appropriate Scripture to older preschoolers in the nursery, and then allow them to march down the aisles of the sanctuary during a worship song, spreading all around the worship center. Ask all women to stand, and then lead preschoolers to repeat their verse for their moms aloud before marching out.

Memory Gift

Ask every woman attending worship to stand. Present each one with a fresh flower or small gift. You could order or make a gift, such as bookmarks, special pins, booklets, or mementos with the church name on it. Ask a church member with poetry talents to write a poem about Christian mothers, copy and distribute it. Use ribbons and cardboard to make Bible place-markers. Each year's small gift can be unique and meaningful.

Presenters

If your church gives token gifts on Mother's Day, vary the presenters each year. The presenters should be recruited ahead of time, and should be old enough to accomplish the task efficiently. Examples: teen boys, fifth graders, older men, new members, ushers.

Baby Dedication

Mother's Day is a great day to schedule a baby dedication ceremony.

Baptism

Many people who aren't Christians attend church with their mother on Mother's Day. Schedule a baptism on that day to demonstrate a clear witness.

Oldest/Youngest

Not to be a fuddy-duddy, but pointing out the oldest and youngest moms during worship isn't a great idea. Some churches present a gift to the mother with the most children, but these days that often involves blended families and may be embarrassing to them. Consider recognizing the mother who has been a Christian the longest, the mother with the newest baby, or even the tallest mother! One year you might ask all mothers who have a new baby this past year to stand and then offer a prayer for all mothers and for those in particular. Or invite ladies to stand briefly if they have children, grandchildren, great-grandchildren, then great-great-grandchildren. Or recognize mothers of preschoolers, elementary-aged children, teens, then those with adult children.

Teen Guy's Video

Ask teenage boys in your church to work together to prepare a brief video to honor their mothers. Play it as a preservice video during morning worship.

Mother's Day Picnic

Plan a casual, catered picnic at a local park for Mother's Day. Ask church members to make reservations for themselves and family members who will attend, and order food from a deli or restaurant so moms don't have to cook.

Worship Him, Not Her

Carefully plan to joyfully honor mothers on Mother's Day, but worship only God.

Motto

Got motto?

"My heart is moved by a noble theme."

—Psalms 45:1

A church motto is like a kid's nickname. It gives identity and significance. Some fresh ideas:

"We'll Love You to Life!"

Every church needs a motto. Describe your church's purpose in a few carefully chosen intriguing words, and you've got a church motto. It's an effective motivating tool that doesn't cost a dime. Mottos are often between three and eight words and may use alliteration, unique capitalization, font, or punctuation. The motto may change from year to year, but it becomes a mantra and gives identity to the church for outsiders.

Where to Use Your Church Motto

Wear it out! Use your church motto on every piece of communication that leaves your church. Put it on the Sunday bulletin, church Web site, fax forms, church business cards, church stationery, visitor cards, prayer sheets, telephone message, Sunday morning welcome announcement, bulletin boards, news releases, staff Internet signatures, church sign, church banners, sports uniforms, advertisements, pew pencils, church coffee mugs, church T-shirts.

A Sampler of Church Mottos

Reading other church mottos may help inspire ideas. Some Indiana mottos:
- "Get the Most Out of Life"—Lifeway Community, Noblesville
- "A Fellowship of JOY"—First Baptist, Griffith
- "Your Place for Family, Friends, and Faith"—Calvary Baptist, West Lafayette

- "Come as You Are . . . Leave Changed" (with leaf logo)—New Life Baptist, Avon
- "The Fellowship of Life"—Sunnycrest Baptist, Marion
- "The Family that Cares"—Fall Creek Baptist, Indianapolis
- "Where Relationships Matter"—Northwoods Baptist, Evansville
- "Living Intentionally for Christ"—Lakeside Fellowship SBC, Columbus
- "The church where love lives"—Parkside Baptist, Columbus
- "Joining Hands and Reaching Out"—Smyrna Baptist
- "Where New Life Begins"—Calvary Baptist, Greenwood
- "The end of your search for a friendly church"—Southwood Baptist, Beech Grove
- "A church of ordinary people worshipping an extraordinary God"—Cline Avenue Fellowship, Highland
- "Reaching the World One Heart at a Time"—Western Avenue Baptist, Connersville

New Christian

"I tell you, in the same way, there is joy in the presence of God's angels over one sinner who repents."

—Luke 15:10

When your spouse or child or friend accepts Christ, celebrate!

Share It

It's worth the long-distance bill! Encourage new Christians to call everyone who is important to them to share about this great decision. Call cousins at college, best friends, relatives, teammates, grandparents, and pastors. Who would you call if your child were elected President of the United States? This is *much* more important than that!

Invite Friends to the Baptism

Send an invitation to the baptism ceremony to everyone they know—friends, relatives, coworkers, classmates, teachers, neighbors. Sit together. Smile. Clap. Celebrate! God could use this ordinance to bring others to know him.

Celebrate

We threw a party at our home after each of our children's baptism services. Every person who had any small part in sharing Christ with them was invited. That included friends, coaches, relatives, pastors, babysitters, and teachers at school, choir, missions, and Sunday school. Our child thanked the group for the part they personally had in sharing about Jesus. There were no gifts, just joyful celebration.

Memorialize It

Purchase a Bible to celebrate this day. Imprint the new Christian's name on the cover. On the front page, record the date they accepted Christ and the baptism date. Ask friends who attend the baptism or the celebration to highlight a Scripture that would challenge the new Christian and pen an encouraging word, along with their signature, in the margin beside that Scripture.

Document It

Ask the new Christian to write out a testimony about how he or she met Christ. He or she can write about the time before they accepted Christ, how they accepted Christ, and the difference in their life. Date and laminate the written testimony for an important keepsake. Use a video camera to capture their personal testimony, chatting casually to obtain a clear testimony of his decision. If it is appropriate in your church, ask someone to videotape the baptism and take a still photo as the baptism occurs.

Bulletin Board

Place a bulletin board in a prime location at church with a photo of new Christians baptized for the entire year.

New Church Staff Member

┌ ─ ─ ─ ─ ─ ┐
| Show that new pastor |
 what a great decision
| he made! |
└ ─ ─ ─ ─ ─ ┘

*"Anyone who welcomes a prophet because he is a
prophet will receive a prophet's reward. And anyone
who welcomes a righteous person because he's righteous
will receive a righteous person's reward."*

—Matthew 10:41

Some welcome ideas for a new pastor or church staff member:

Personalized Map

For a perfect gift, mark a city map with the location of the church, the minister's home, schools, favorite restaurants and stores, government buildings, parks, repair shops, dry cleaners, and other key destinations of interest.

Digital Pounding

Welcome a new pastor with an e-pounding! Ask church members to e-mail notes of welcome, encouragement, and prayer. If they do not have a computer, they could e-mail from the local library.

Tuesday at Two

Ask church members individually to commit to pray for the new minister at a specific hour once weekly. For example, Joe commits to pray for the new pastor every Monday morning at 6:00 a.m. during his drive to work. Present the pastor with a time chart of church members who are praying faithfully for him and his ministry. What an encouragement! This idea could be presented to the new pastor from a Sunday school class group, choir, youth group, deacons, etc.

Pastor Steve Davis

For positive impact, print the new pastor's name on the permanent exterior sign and on his office door before his arrival.

Welcome Basket

Prepare a lovely basket full of items that are manufactured in your town. Include a note of greeting with your telephone number, just in case they need something.

Welcome PKs (Pastor's Kids)

Present the pastor's children with a welcome gift from the church. At our new pastorate in Dallas, our kids were given a cowboy hat and a personalized Dallas Cowboys jersey. Suddenly, they were thrilled to be there!

Try My Favorite Restaurant

It's hard work to relocate to a new city. Each Sunday school class could purchase a gift certificate to their favorite restaurant. Print directions to the restaurant, along with notes about your favorite foods there.

Welcome Notes

Distribute the minister's current address and ask members to send brief notes of prayer and greeting before he moves to town.

Pound 'em

One church gave us an old-fashioned pounding. That means every member brought some nonperishable food to fill up our food pantry. It not only helped our grocery budget that first month, but it made our teenage sons ecstatic.

Freshen Up

A vase of fresh flowers says "Welcome." Clean the pastor's office meticulously. If fresh paint, carpet, or furniture is needed, consult the incoming pastor for color preferences.

Name Tags

For a really kind gesture, make name tags for every church member to wear for several months after the new minister arrives.

New Construction

"It was in my heart to build a house for the name of the LORD my God."

—1 Chronicles 22:7b

Ministry can't wait until the building is complete. Need fresh ideas for ministry during construction?

Coming Soon

As soon as construction begins, place a sign on the property to inform those passing by. It can let them know what's coming and how to find where your church is meeting right now.

Cross on Top

Ever notice that many construction projects put a tree on the top floor during construction? Why not give this tradition a Christian twist? If the building is multistory, top the construction project with a large cross made of two-by-fours.

Plumbers Lunch Bell

Church members could prepare an occasional brown-bag lunch or hot lunch for construction workers as a special treat. Present each worker with a note of encouragement, a drawing by a young Sunday school class, or a small gift. Include a witness tract and an invitation to worship with your church. Using a schedule from the general contractor, church members can plan a lunch or snack for every different work crew, i.e., painters, electricians, landscapers.

Rafter Writing

When the framing is complete for the building, have a private worship service onsite for members only. Form a circle around the building walls for prayer time, and then distribute permanent markers to everyone. Play a worshipful Christian music CD as each person finds a stud or rafter and prayerfully writes his or her name along with a prayer or Scripture on it.

Teen Tribute

Teens could dig a hole and plant a tree in an appropriate place on the property.

Steeple Setting Ceremony

If your new building plans include a steeple or a cross, plan an informal celebration for members at the time of its placement on the building.

Weekly Photo Update

The preservice audiovisual at your church can include a couple of photos of progress on the new building each week during construction.

Building Photographer

Designate at least one person to take photos of the building and workers during the coming project. They can submit occasional photographs to a local newspaper for possible publication, prepare a photo journal of the project to unveil at the building dedication, and select several action photos to use for building updates in church newsletters, on the church Web site and weekly preservice audiovisuals. Challenge the photographer to capture a photograph of every volunteer worker and every phase of the project.

Sweeping Senior Saints

Form a "Triple S" club of senior adults who will volunteer to do a weekly cleanup of the building site. Working with the building contractor, they can clean, pick up, and sweep the area; and they may save significant cleanup cost during the building project.

Shovel Ceremony

See "Groundbreaking" on page 80.

New Member Assimilation

"Now you are the body of Christ, and individual members of it."

—1 Corinthians 12:27

They didn't join your church to watch. Help new church members find their own place of ministry within the body. Need fresh ideas?

Dinner with the Pastor

Ask new members to sit at the pastor's table if your church serves Wednesday evening dinners. Our church presented a printed invitation for them to come to a complimentary meal with the pastor. A special table was prepared, with name cards at the place setting for the new members. If the new members did not completely fill the pastor's table, church members from their age group were invited ahead of time to join them.

Spiritual Gifts Evaluation

As part of the new member packet, include a form to help new church members discover their spiritual gift. Include a stamped envelope addressed to the pastor, and ask the new member to complete the survey and mail it within a week. A second survey, listing opportunities for using their gifts within the church, can allow them to volunteer for service. Make a goal of helping every new church member find at least a small place of service in the church within a month. Some simple "starter" ministries for newcomers: greeter, library, usher, prayer chapel, etc.

New Member Gift

New members at our church were presented with a church membership packet which includes a church directory, a magnet with church telephone numbers, e-mail contacts, a family ticket for a free dinner with the pastor at Wednesday night's supper, and a license plate cover with the church name and logo for their cars.

Smile!

Take a digital photo of new church members immediately after they join. Before they leave the counseling room or church building, snap it! Send a digital photograph by e-mail to the new church member's Sunday school teacher.

I'm Accepted

Make regular updates, including photographs, for the church pictorial directory. It helps old members know new members and helps new members feel accepted. Present an updated church directory to new members.

Bulletin Board Photo

Create a bulletin board for photos of new church members along with names of their family members.

Another Photo

Print a photo of new church members in the church newsletter or bulletin.

Prayer Photo

Place a digital photograph of new church members as a screen saver of the church computer, and pray for that new member each time his or her photograph passes.

Annual Harvest Dinner

Consider planning an annual Harvest Dinner near the Thanksgiving season to celebrate all that God has done during the past year. Specifically recognize every new church member from the past year, using photos and special name tags.

Sunday School Assignment

Automatically enroll every new church member in an appropriate Sunday school class. Leaders from that class should contact new members immediately to help assimilate them. New members are welcome, of course, to choose a different class if they prefer, but they should receive invitations to Bible study from at least one class immediately.

They Need Me!

A new church member should receive multiple invitations immediately after they join: an invitation to women's, men's, children, youth groups, and events; an invitation to sing in the choir or praise team; an invitation to take an hour in the prayer chapel; an invitation to use the church library; an invitation to Sunday school or small group Bible study. You get the idea. Ascertain that new church members know they're welcome and needed.

New Member Luncheon

Many churches plan quarterly receptions or luncheons to welcome all new members to the church. Invite the Sunday school director for each new member's class to host the table where they'll sit. Our church's luncheon was planned for Sunday after church, and a brief orientation informed new members about important events and projects of the church.

Membership 101

Give your church membership inquiry class a special name, such as Connection Class, Fresh Start, or Discovery Class. A class series could be titled Membership 101, 201, and 301.

Special Location

Location for a membership class is important. It could be in a church parlor, the nicest church classroom, a nearby restaurant's private dining room, the home of the pastor or staff member, or at a nice picnic on the church lawn.

Who Attends the Membership Class?

New church members and guests who are considering joining a church may attend. The more the merrier! Many churches require membership class attendance for new church members.

Who Leads the Membership Class?

The membership class could be taught by the pastor, a staff member, a minister's wife, a deacon, a married couple, or a single adult. The teacher should be a church member who is a gifted teacher and has been recommended by the pastor.

When Is the New Members Class?

Every church's membership class is different. Some have lunch on Sunday, with a two-hour class afterward. Others offer a four-week, one-hour class on Sunday morning or evening, a weekday evening, or a Saturday morning. Just make the time fit your church's schedule. It is important to offer the class several times each year. Offer it often, multiplying the possibilities for newcomers to attend.

What Happens at the Membership Class?

The key goal of the class is to help new members and potential new members feel knowledgeable about church beliefs and policies and to feel comfortable and assimilated into the church. Topics may include church doctrine, history, ordinances, mission strategy, goals, membership data, organization structure, ministries of the church, and opportunities for service. The class will explain opportunities and expectations of members for discipleship, ministry, tithing, witness training, and ministry opportunities. If potential members are included in the class, share God's plan of salvation and information about how to join the church. The class should be well prepared, using a variety of teaching techniques and multiple handouts. Our church's membership class included a tour of the church. Whew! But worth the effort.

The Results

A quality membership class will help to assimilate new members and educate potential members. Better knowledge will produce commitment to ministries, missions, discipleship, stewardship, and outreach. Membership cards are distributed during the class for those who desire to join.

Want Ads

Print a weekly or monthly "help wanted" classified section in the church newsletter or bulletin, listing various opportunities for service within the church. Include short-term and long-term opportunities. Update the list regularly, including ministries such as audiovisual, orchestra, greeters for a special event, regular greeters, Web site management, or office volunteer.

Bullets

Use bullets beside ministry opportunities listed in the church bulletin. Supply a tear-off section and invite people to check their interests and place the paper in the offering plate as a gift to God.

Response Cards

Response cards in the pew envelope holder can offer a regular opportunity for worshippers to volunteer to assist with needs within the church. For example, "We will be painting our baby nursery at the church on Friday and Saturday. If you can help, please indicate your interest on the ministry response card, place it in the offering plate today, and we will contact you."

Under Their Feet

Remind worshippers of an important upcoming event by writing announcements on the church sidewalks using colorful sidewalk chalks. Example: "The Great Revival begins Monday at 7:00 p.m. Who will you invite?" This is a great ministry for teens to undertake.

It's Personal

The best way to involve people is through personal invitation, even if it's barely personal. For example: ladies at worship exits distributing an invitation to the annual ladies' brunch.

Survey, Then Call

As part of their new member packet, include a survey to inquire about the new member's talents, experience, and interests. Provide a stamped envelope addressed to the pastor at the church, and follow up with a telephone call if the survey is not received. When the survey is returned, forward the member's name to the appropriate leaders where he or she may serve in the church. Then assure that the new member receives at least one invitation to serve immediately.

Ministry Fair

Your church's annual missions and ministry fair can offer sign-up sheets for many ministries in the church at their exhibits. Ascertain that every new member attends the event, and encourage each one to find a place of service in the church.

New Year

┌ ─ ─ ─ ─ ┐
│ *Begin the New Year* │
│ *with a bang!* │
└ ─ ─ ─ ─ ┘

"You crown the year with Your goodness."

—Psalms 65:11

Celebrate a new year with your closest Christian friends. Need fresh ideas?

24-Hour New Year Project

Here's a life-changing bring-in-the-new-year project: Ring in the New Year by reading the entire New Testament aloud as a church. It's exciting and meaningful. It takes about twenty-four hours to read the entire New Testament, so register members for ninety-six fifteen-minute shifts or forty-eight half hour shifts. Begin at 5:00 p.m. December 31st and read until 5:00 p.m. January 1st. Make a huge scheduling chart, and involve everyone—children, senior adults, teens, couples, singles, families, new Christians. Purchase a large Bible for the pulpit, and print instructions for each reader to pen their signature in the margin where they begin reading. As new readers arrive, they begin reading where the last person stopped. If you've completed the New Testament before the twenty-four hours is completed, continue reading Proverbs and Psalms. The Bible can be placed in the library afterward. Make an audio recording of the Bible reading to share with shut-ins. Invite church members and members of the community to stop by to listen anytime during the twenty-four hours.

New Year's Resolutions

Encouraging your class or church to make meaningful New Year's commitments to grow as a Christian? Ask each person to write his or her specific commitments to God and seal it inside a self-addressed envelope. Mail the unopened resolutions to them on March 1 for a reminder and encouragement.

New Year's Video

Create a video of highlights of church blessings and events during last year. Emphasize discipleship, new Bible classes, baptisms, new members, church plants, and other accomplishments that fit your church's goals. The video may be used as a looped presentation on televisions in church foyers, as handout DVDs for guests, and for special New Year's celebration events.

Midnight Party Merge

If several groups in your church plan New Year's parties, why not plan a huge "Party Merge" at the stroke of midnight? Ask everyone to arrive outside the church (or inside if the weather's bad), distribute candles or sparklers, and have an encouraging word of prayer to bring in the new year. Then fellowship and celebrate God's blessing of a new year to serve him.

New Year's Resolution

If your church or Sunday school class has taken a challenge to read through the Bible this year, plan an awards ceremony to present certificates to those who succeeded. One church displayed a huge Plexiglas grid with names of those taking the challenge. Across the top were printed the names of each book of the Bible, and members placed an X on each book they completed. My favorite new resource for yearly Bible reading is "The Every Day with Jesus Bible."

Nursing Home Ministry

> ```
> And with that hug,
> share Jesus.
> ```

"The splendor of old men is gray hair."

—Proverbs 20:29

They're waiting. Need fresh ideas for effective nursing home ministry?

Manicure Team

They show up at the nursing home each Tuesday at 10:00 a.m. with their plastic totes full of polish and nail files. Every week a long row of ladies wait in a row of wheelchairs and walkers behind each nail table. No, they're not professional nail technicians. They're just our team of Christian ladies from a local church, ready to minister with a listening ear, a gentle touch, nail polish, and a prayer.

Monthly Birthday Party

Make every resident feel special by planning a party each month for nursing home residents with birthdays. Stock a portable party box with balloons, streamers, and birthday plates and napkins. Take a cake or cupcakes, and you're ready. Offer a prayer and Scripture for the birthday honorees.

Adopt a Grandparent

Teens, children, or adults in your church can make a yearlong commitment to make weekly visits to their adopted "grandparent." A nursing home director will happily provide names of residents who need visitors.

Banana Bingo

Residents never tired of it. For years members from our church played bingo each week at a nursing home with bananas for the prize.

Lord's Supper

Deacons from our church administered the Lord's Supper to our members in nursing homes each quarter. Members of our adult and youth choirs divided into trios and quartets and accompanied the deacons for the ordinance once each year.

Women on Mission

For many years, Betsy Moore, wife of retired Indiana Baptist Executive Director E. Harmon Moore, led a Women on Mission class at their retirement community. The attendance was great, and the group was vibrant.

Bible Study

With the nursing home director's permission, schedule a weekly Bible study for residents. You could use a rotating list of teachers or the same teacher each week. You could plan a topical Bible study series, teaching biblical answers to relevant questions, such as: How can I get into heaven? How do we lean on God? or What does heaven look like? Advertise the topic each week.

Story Time

Announce a live story time at the nursing home. Read selected Bible stories. Read a weekly devotional book. Choose a novel with a Christian theme, and read a chapter weekly along with a chapter from God's Word.

Read Through the Bible

If you are committed to a weekly visit at the nursing home, consider reading through the Bible. If you read a half hour weekly, you could complete the New Testament, Psalms, and Proverbs in less than a year. Use a chart to mark off chapters for listeners to view progress. Read with enthusiasm for the story that has truly changed the world.

Penmanship

Write letters for residents you visit. Or help them write a weekly journal entry in a book for them. Or spend several sessions writing or recording memoirs.

Centerpieces

A group of talented ladies from your church could create Christmas center-pieces for dining tables at the nursing home. If they're industrious, they could make centerpieces for several holidays.

Touch of Sunshine

Can your nursing home ministry team place a birdbath or bird feeder near the nursing home's window or patio? Or plant flowers? Then you can bring bird food when you visit.

Worship

Sundays without corporate worship would be heartbreaking. Plan a weekly service for the nursing home, complete with sermon, music, and an evangelistic invitation. A retired pastor would be effective in this setting.

Hymn Sing-along

Always a gigantic hit! It can be as simple as one pianist leading the group, or you can bring an entire ensemble or choir and lots of instruments.

Develop Relationships

By visiting the same hallway or individuals at the nursing home every week, you'll begin to learn names and needs. Always ask the residents if they would like for you to pray with them before you leave. Young ladies from our church made seasonal door decorations for residents on their hallway. They became known as the "door darlings." Corny? Yes. Effective? Very.

And with That Hug . . .

Share Jesus. Never forget that many of the residents of any nursing home are not Christians. They need more than good deeds and smiles. They desperately need to know Jesus personally. Make a point to know the spiritual condition of each person you visit. Then share God's plan of salvation.

Offering

"For God loves a cheerful giver."

—2 Corinthians 9:7

It's an important part of worship. Treat it that way!

Lots of Ushers

The usher coordinator should include many volunteer ushers, using a rotation system or varying usher assignments for different services. They should recruit new ushers often. Since ushering can be an entry-level ministry, allow new Christians or new church members to serve.

Variety of Ushers

Use a wide age-range of ushers from older teens to senior adults, various races, new Christians, old Christians. Ushers are a visual representation of your church, and guests will pay particular attention to them. This is a great visual demonstration of how God loves and uses all people!

Stewardship Scripture

Add joy to giving by quoting Scripture. Select a favorite stewardship Scripture, and lead the congregation to quote it joyfully before the offertory each Sunday. Project it as an audiovisual, but encourage members to memorize it. For example, Pastor Jim McGinlay at First Baptist Church Lakeside, Lake Worth, Texas, uses this Scripture weekly:

> "Now therefore, our God, we give You thanks and praise Your glorious name. But who am I, and who are my people that we should be able to give as generously as this? For everything comes from You, we have given You only what comes from Your own hand."
> (1 Chron. 29:13–14)

It's awesome to watch children and adults quoting that verse as the offering plate is passed.

Choir Givers

Don't forget to pass the offering plate to choir members so they can participate in the privilege of tithing as an act of worship.

Ushers on Youth Sunday

For special emphases day at church, such as children's day, singles day, or senior adult day, wouldn't it be appropriate to have some of those people act as ushers that Sunday?

Sing and Sacrifice

At some churches worshippers stand and sing during the offertory. At others the choir or praise team presents a worshipful offertory song as ushers collect the offering. Instrumentalists could play a special music arrangement. Still other churches encourage worshippers to bring their monetary offerings to the front of the worship center and place them in a container as an act of worship.

Reverse Order

Occasionally vary your method slightly. For instance, ushers may begin at the rear pew, passing the plate from the back row to the front.

Altar Presentation

At some churches, ushers reverently bring the offering plates to the altar after passing the plates.

Beginning, Middle, or End?

Giving can be celebrated at various times during worship: during choir or solo music, just after the invitation and before introducing new members, at the end of the service, or during a worshipful instrumental moment before the sermon.

Buckets or Bags

Different churches use large baskets, bags, bowls, or offering plates. They can be wood, fabric, wicker, plastic, or silver. Make the collection utensil fit your church.

Stationery Box

Some churches don't pass any container for the offering. They use an attractive box at the rear of the worship area where worshippers place the gifts as they enter or depart.

Joash Chest

For a one-day special offering, a deacon at our church built a beautiful wooden "Joash chest," which was placed at the front of the worship center. Members filed by to place their offering in the chest (see 2 Chron. 24:8–14).

Usher Annual Party

Ushers at our church held a chili party each January for all ushers and their spouses. The usher coordinator gave a brief appreciation speech, and the rest of the party was strictly for fellowship.

Outreach

"And off he went, proclaiming throughout the town all that Jesus had done for him."

—Luke 8:39

Create an atmosphere of joy and anticipation for outreach. Need fresh ideas?

Take Five

If your church doesn't have a regular weekly outreach night, choose five consecutive weeks during fall and five during spring, and plan outreach evenings during weeks your church probably has the most visitors.

Choices

Why not offer several choices for church members who come for weekly outreach? In additional to making personal outreach visits, some attenders could make telephone calls, write cards, pray for prospects, or send e-mail notes.

My Card

Print inexpensive business cards for members to use for formal and informal outreach. Include your church name, logo, address, phone, Web site, pastor's name, and worship times. A blank line at the bottom can be signed by the church member, and the byline beneath it could read, "Every member a minister" or "church member." God's plan of salvation could be printed on the back of the cards.

Weekly Outreach

Three simple items can help make your church's weekly outreach successful: a whiteboard, a clock, and a coffeepot. As members arrive to make outreach visits, send them out with current assignments almost immediately (the clock).

No dawdling or confusion. No long premeeting. Just pair them in teams, distribute assignments, and send them out. The report-back time should be the time for fellowship and celebration (the coffeepot). As they return from visits, chart the results (the whiteboard) to create excitement and celebration for God's blessings for the evening.

The 3/3 Rule

Here's a good rule of thumb for first-time guests at church: within three hours after worship, they receive a telephone call. A friendly member may want to call the entire list each Sunday afternoon. Our church's deacons made a quick phone call just to say thanks for worshipping with us and to ask if guests had any questions or needs. Within three days of their visit, they should receive an in-home visit.

Six Family Members/Six Invitations

Each family member who visited should receive some type of contact from their Sunday school or age-group division. If you have a quality women's ministry, someone from that group may call to invite a woman to an event. A teen may call their teenager to ask them to a Wednesday teen event at church. A children's minister or children's worker may call a second-grader. A preschool worker may call the mother to inquire about how their preschooler enjoyed class. Don't worry about overkill. Personal, caring contact is the most effective outreach.

Include Children in Outreach

When making visits to homes of visitors with children, why not take along your child? Kids can help with outreach if your church does reverse trick-or-treating. Or if child care is offered on outreach night, older children could write welcome notes to visitors their age that attended church last week.

Road-Trip Outreach Event

This outreach event involves lots of people and will have a party-type atmosphere. Use it for Vacation Bible School follow-up or after a well-attended church event when you have lots of prospects to visit. Recruit church members with station wagons, vans, or SUVs as drivers. Prepare trip itineraries (the afternoon's schedule) and road maps marked with several visitation assignments in the same area of town. A pile of suitcases and a "Road Trip" banner greet church members as they arrive. Each team of visitors takes a suitcase containing visitation assignments and makes several visits before joining the group at a local park for ice cream and celebration.

Connection Day

Teens love this. Members of a Sunday school department invite friends to church for a high-attendance "Friends Day." Each member's guests are tied in a row to him, wrist to wrist, to form a line. Those who bring lots of guests are definitely noticed! This could be done for a fifth-grade class or an entire youth group.

Welcome Gift

Deliver a small welcome gift and invitation to worship to new move-ins in your community. Gift ideas: Coffee mug with church name and worship times imprinted. Refrigerator magnet. An item manufactured in your town. Something that represents your town, i.e. corn on the cob in Indiana, chips and hot sauce in San Antonio, or homemade jam. Two homebound members of our church prepared and froze breads for newcomer deliveries.

Moving Van Watch

Members of our church watched for moving vans arriving in their neighborhood, and called the church immediately. A team responded with an immediate visit, delivering homemade cake or cookies and an invitation to worship on Sunday.

Parking Lot

"What road leads to the place where light is dispersed?"

—Job 38:24

Even a parking lot can help point people to Jesus. Some fresh ideas:

Guest Parking Signs

Use professionally painted signs to clearly mark parking spots near the main church entrance for first-time guests. (Second-time guests are on their own!) This not only helps simplify their visit but also helps your greeters identify and welcome first-timers.

Parking Entrance Signs

Parking lot entrance and exit signs can set the tone. Examples:
- Enter to Worship. Depart to Serve.
- You are entering Holy Ground. You are entering your mission field.
- Welcome to First Baptist Church. Welcome to your mission field.
- Whosoever will may come. The chosen of God.

Which Door?

Can a newcomer easily find the church entrance from any parking space?

Name a Lot

If your parking lot is large or confusing, consider "naming" the lots, using colored flags or professional signs. Then a newcomer can easily identify the correct lot. You could use titles such as the fruits of the spirit (love, joy, peace, etc.) or biblical references or names.

Stripes

Restripe your church parking lot occasionally. It makes the entire facility look clean and fresh and, properly planned, may even add additional spaces. Some community planning departments will sketch the parking spaces as a complimentary service.

Parking Space Shortage

Your church can't keep growing if you're out of parking. Could your church borrow or rent adjacent parking from a bank, school, or business that doesn't use their lot on Sunday?

Prime Real Estate

Encourage church leaders and regular attenders to joyfully park in the farthest parking spaces, leaving more convenient parking spaces for elderly, parents of small children, and newcomers.

Fore

If your church parking lot is large or inconvenient, you might use friendly volunteers in golf carts to transport people.

Easter Parking

If your church is planning for extra worship services and extra crowds on Easter or other special Sundays, consider borrowing nearby parking. If the parking lot is full, those guests will drive on by. Each Easter Sunday our church rented a bus and borrowed the high school parking lot, a few blocks from the church. Regular attenders gladly arrived early and took the bus so guests could find parking nearby.

Personal Evangelism

*It's news.
And it's good.*

"If I say: I won't mention Him or speak any longer in His name, His message becomes a fire burning in my heart, shut up in my bones."

—Jeremiah 20:9

Fresh ideas to challenge the church to share Jesus.

The Challenge

Use a commitment card on the first Sunday of the new year to challenge every church member to personally share his or her faith with at least one person this year.

"Fire in My Bones" Mini-Conference

Plan a one-night conference with one purpose: to teach and ignite Christians to share Jesus. Offer several choices of short how-to classes, such as how to use a marked testament, FAITH, power band, Roman Road, EvangeCube, friendship evangelism, evangelistic Christmas tea, witness bracelets, and how to write out your testimony. Use numerous handouts. Order matchbooks printed with the church name and with the words "Fire in my Bones." For the closing moments, ask each attender to take a matchbook as their indication of a commitment to tell someone about Jesus every week this month.

Lunch with a Purpose

Encourage every church member to make a list of friends, relatives, and coworkers who don't know Christ, then systematically take each one to lunch and share his or her personal testimony with them.

Auto-Witness

Encourage church members to watch for everyday ways to witness. Christians can place a Scripture on their car's dash for passengers to read. A church bumper sticker or license plate cover could open a door for a witness. Add a word of witness to your telephone answering machine message. Choose an e-mail address that shines for Christ. For example, my e-mail address is jesuslivesindiana (Get it? Indiana/in Diana).

Printed Witness

Encourage church members to add a Scripture to their printed bank checks and be ready to share Christ when someone comments about it. They can order boxes of personal business cards with the plan of salvation printed on the back. Encourage church members to share Christian books and music CDs with unsaved friends. My friend, Gwen, became a Christian as a young adult by reading a Christian novel.

Water Cooler Witness

Challenge church members to be an active witness every day at work, finding opportunities to tell about how Jesus makes a difference in his or her life. People everywhere are dying to know Him.

Silent Witness

Challenge church members to use their home and office décor as a witness by using Christian symbols and Scripture. If it is possible, they could keep a Bible in their work area, Christian books on their shelf, and a Christian witness on their screen saver.

A Tract in My Pocket

Help church members find a witnessing tool that works for them. Teach them to use a favorite witnessing tract, and provide tracts for church members to keep in their desk, toolbox, backpack, glove box, computer case, workout bag or pocket. Some will use a marked New Testament, a salvation bracelet, or an EvangeCube. My daughter kept an EvangeCube on her coffee table during college and had no choice but to tell the story of Jesus when guests asked. Find a favorite evangelistic Web site, e-mail it to church members, and ask them to bookmark it to use as a witness.

Small-Sized Bible

Encourage church members to buy a small Bible that will fit in a pocket, backpack, or handbag and keep it with them at all times. They'll be surprised how often they'll use it.

It's Great at My Church

Encourage church members to do more than just tell work associates and friends *about* their church. Many people are just waiting for an invitation.

The Stroller Ministry

Remind church members that their phase of life can open doors for sharing Christ. Kids in sports? They're in the "bleacher ministry." Retiree? They're in the fishing ministry or garage sale ministry or camper ministry. High-rise employee? They're in the "elevator ministry."

"In a Minute We're Going to Pray"

You say to your waitress, "Is there something we can pray for you about?" Then do it sincerely. Carry witnessing tracts to leave with your tip.

Do the Dot

John Rogers, evangelism director for Indiana Baptists, uses this method often. Place a small red dot over the number 2 on your watch. Remind yourself to share with someone by 2:00 p.m. daily. Others will ask why the dot is on your watch, and this will open the door for you to share. Share that Jesus died more than two thousand years ago. The red symbolizes his blood shed for us.

Do the Diamond

(My girl version of the "dot.") Buy tiny nail gems at the drug store. Place one "diamond" on your pinkie or forefinger nail, and add several coats of clear polish. Each time you notice it, ask yourself, "Am I shining for Jesus right now?" It may help you to notice a witnessing opportunity. If people comment on it, tell them it reminds you that God saved you and gives you a reason to shine.

Prayer

"Be persistent in prayer."

—Romans 12:12

A church without prayer is like a Porsche without gas—good looking but not much power. Some fresh ideas:

Church Staff Prayer

Our church staff prayed each Monday for every prayer request submitted at our church. They signed a nice greeting card stating they prayed for the need and mailed it to a few of the most urgent requests each week.

Web Site Prayer Requests

Allow viewers to submit a prayer request on your church Web site.

Pew Prayer Requests

Cards may be placed in the pew's envelope holders inviting attenders to submit prayer requests for the church prayer list or for staff prayer time only.

Clipboard Prayer Requests

If your church uses a clipboard registration for each pew, place a blank on the form for prayer requests.

Prayer Partners

Want to assign prayer partners for your Bible class or church? Take a Polaroid or digital photo of each attender as they arrive, and attach a small magnet to the back. Place men and women photos in two separate baskets. Draw photos out of a basket in twos to pair prayer partners for the year. Each person takes his or her partner's photograph as a prayer reminder.

Mega-Prayer for the City

Plan well ahead to implement this prayer emphasis. Use a large city map. Place one-inch stick-on dots around the edges, spaced slightly apart. Ask church members to sign their name on a dot, which will indicate the approximate location where they will pray. Schedule a specific time, such as a Saturday morning at 10:00 a.m., when everyone will physically go to their location in the city to pray. They may kneel or stand or stroll or sit. Don't specify a required time limit, but know that God is listening to his people pray!

Pray in the New Year

Open the church worship center on New Year's Eve, and invite church members to stop by for a few minutes between 6:00 p.m. and midnight to pray. Assign six groups of deacons or church leaders to oversee one of the six hours.

Prayer Around the School

A similar event could be planned for youth, youth leaders, and youth parents to pray for their school.

Monthly Prayer Calendar

Create a monthly prayer calendar with the name of one church family, a staff member or church leader, and one ministry of the church written on each day of the month. Challenge members to pray each day for those requests.

Can My Church Staff a Prayer Chapel?

Of course you can! A prayer chapel that's staffed 24-7 is fabulous, but most churches don't start there. Consider staffing a prayer chapel for one twelve-hour period each Monday. Twelve church members commit to pray for one hour each week. For example, Joe prays from 6:00 to 7:00 a.m. each Monday. Stan prays from 7:00 to 8:00 a.m., etc. Or staff the prayer chapel from 6:00 a.m. to noon on Saturday. By asking church members to commit to pray for a regular one-hour period each week, you may gradually increase it to 24-7!

Where's the Prayer Chapel?

If your church has no prayer room, consider creating one from an out-of-the way closet or storage room. Clean and paint the room, then have a "Prayer Chapel" sign professionally done. If a church member does stained glass, commission a piece to decorate the wall or a window.

Furnishing the Prayer Chapel

Create a lovely, comfortable place to spend time with God. A door hanger can state, "Somebody's praying!" Furnish the room with a desk, chair, and kneeling bench. Stock the desk with a Bible, church directory, local phone book, missionary information, stationery, pens, tissues, and a CD player with a choice of Christian music. Place a city map on one wall and a world map on another.

Organizing Prayer Requests

A prayer request notebook in your prayer chapel should list each prayer request, date requested, person making the request, update information, and date the prayer was answered. Add new pages to the front of the book, and place a marker so each person may begin praying where the last prayer left off. Create a Rolodex of long-term prayer requests. A notebook can list names of local, state, and national leaders; missionaries; church leaders, etc. for prayer.

What Will I Do in the Prayer Chapel?

Create a page with suggestions for church members for their prayer chapel hour. Time can be spent praising God, praying for current prayer requests, praying for long-term prayer requests, praying for missionaries, praying Scripture, praying for church members, singing, drawing, kneeling. When the next person arrives to continue the prayer chain, say a brief prayer with him or her before leaving.

Prayer Labyrinth

You may prefer to set up a permanent or one-day prayer labyrinth, with multiple prayer stations. Several different walls or areas of the room are carefully designed for specific prayer. Soft worship music plays as Christians stop by to pray for minutes or hours. Examples: One corner may have a kneeling bench. Post a world map on a wall with a listing or book of missionaries supported by your church. Another wall could have a computer-generated list of every church member's name with instructions for those praying to initial beside names as they pray for them. A table could have markers and papers, asking people to write names for God as they pray, posting them on a collage-type display. An area covered in butcher paper could have art supplies to encourage artistic prayer expression. A Bible on a stand, open to a specific Scripture, can have instructions to read that Scripture and respond to God in an open notebook. The possibilities for a prayer labyrinth are vast.

Preservice Audiovisual

They'll come to church early just to see this.

"From Him the whole body, fitted and knit together by every supporting ligament, promotes the growth of the body for building up itself in love by the proper working of each individual part."

—Ephesians 4:16

Technology brings "announcement time" to a new dimension.

Inform, Welcome, Remind, Encourage

A preservice audiovisual projection with music can inform, welcome, remind, and encourage early arrivers at Sunday worship services. Some ideas include:

- Announcements of upcoming events
- Accomplishment announcements, i.e. fifth-grade Sunday school set record attendance last week
- Announcement of new Sunday school classes to begin
- Church vision statement, motto, theme, church Web site
- Invitation to Sunday school
- Welcome note to guests
- Invitation to join choir or orchestra
- Today's schedule
- Scripture verse or this year's theme Scripture
- Missionary statistics
- Child-care announcement
- Photos of last week's church activities
- Photos of new church members

- Photos of members baptized today
- Photos of church staff members, labeled with their name and position
- Photos of deacons
- Photos of Sunday school teachers
- Photos of Sunday school classes
- Photos of missionaries
- Photos of our mission church and mission pastor
- Photos of a recent mission trip or ministry project
- Update photos of a church construction project

Sermon

It's surprisingly simple to create first-class projection of sermon outlines, visuals, clips, and fill-in-the-blanks for sermons. Many listeners' learning retention increases substantially with visual aids. Clueless? Ask a teenager for help.

Video Clips

Motivational and informative video clips are available from state conventions, the North American Mission Board, and the International Mission Board. Many clips are just minutes long and quite effective.

Video on Special Emphasis Sundays

Prepare unique personalized audiovisuals to enhance special emphasis Sundays. Show it during preservice, offertory, music, or as part of the sermon. For example, a slide show of father/daughter photos could show during an appropriate song on Father's Day. Photos of graduates could congratulate seniors. Couples photos with subtitles like "Joe and Sarah Smith, married 17 years" could help celebrate Valentine's Day. Informal interviews with five-year-olds could relate what they're thankful for on Thanksgiving. Prepare a brief video to honor church members who are teachers and school employees when school begins. Show photos of all new babies born since last Mother's Day. Photos of members in military could be shown on a patriotic Sunday. Show a short clip of your church youth doing tug-of-war to illustrate a sermon point. Show action photos of various Sunday school classes to promote high attendance day. Show mission trip photos during a mission testimony or women's retreat photos synced to a Christian song.

The Brains behind the Ministry

A tech team at your church can bring new interest and vitality to worship. Recognize them. Pray for them. Encourage them. Buy them matching visors or shirts or bags. What a joy to use every ability to serve our Lord!

Revivals

┌ — — — — — ┐
│ *Prepare like heaven* │
│ *depends on it. For* │
│ *somebody, it does.* │
└ — — — — — ┘

"Will You not revive us again so that Your people may rejoice in You?"

—Psalms 85:6

There's nothing "business as usual" about a revival. Need fresh ideas?

Title It

Work with your evangelist to choose a title to entice non-Christians. Call it the "Never Too Late" revival, "The Ignition Conference," "Get Real," "Is That All There Is? Seminar." You get the idea. An artistic member could design a logo.

Just One

Urge church members to pray for just one lost friend, invite them to dinner at their home, and then bring them to the revival.

Countdown

Show your excitement! A huge countdown sign outside the church can show a daily countdown: "31 days until 'Never Too Late' Revival begins!"

Business Cards

Print inexpensive business cards for revival invitations. Give handfuls to church members for their friends.

Personal E-Invitations

Design intriguing e-invitations for church members to send their entire e-mail address book.

Tell the Town

Use all available media to invite your city. Write articles for the local newspaper, use cable television community notices, yard signs, mail, television, and radio. Ask the local grocery if you can provide flyers for grocery bags.

Name That Pew

The old "pack a pew" still works! Designate each night to highlight a specific group. Make signs as groups arrive to place on the ends of their pews. For example, Monday could be Sunday school night, with all classes attempting to pack several pews with their friends. Tuesday might be neighbors night, when members bring people on their block. Other services could reach relatives, friends, seniors, singles, teens, work associates, kids, bowling teams—you name it! Plan music, drama, and message to reach that audience.

Special Emphasis, Special Plans

Don't plan your regular music on senior adult night. Bring out that old-time religion and have fun with it. The music, drama, and message for special evenings can be geared to that crowd. An appropriate special enticement may be offered to fit the theme. Youth night must have free pizza. Kids night could feature puppets, and neighbors night could end with a coffee and cake fellowship. Make it fit your church, but pack 'em in to hear about Jesus nightly.

Call the Town

Throw a tele-party, using land lines and cell phones to call and invite hundreds on your church prospect list and inactive file. If it's appropriate in your area, attempt to call the whole local phone book! Make it fun with balloons and signs and food. When a caller talks to someone who plans to attend, he hangs up, then rings a bell, and writes a mark on a sign up front. Revival is no game, but it's amazing how effective a simple telephone invitation can be.

Door Hangers

Be sure everyone who lives nearby your church has an invitation by making door-hanger invitations. Youth might take this as an outreach project. Would church members actually invite the people who live on their block? Give them some door hangers and challenge them.

Made You Look

Rent a searchlight or hot-air balloon sign. Wrap your entire church building as a giant gift for the "Just for You Revival." Flock your churchyard with plastic flamingos for the "One Leg to Stand On" revival and put flamingo revival signs in members' yards or businesses. Print revival T-shirts to wear ahead of time, i.e. "Follow Me To The 'Which Way? Revival.'" Gear all promotion to the people you want to reach for Christ.

Simultaneous Prayer Walk

Plan a simultaneous prayer walk, with each church member prayer-walking his or her neighborhood or work or influence area on the same day.

Cottage Prayer

Schedule prayer meetings in church members' homes, with one home available in each area of town. Distribute maps marking the locations.

Fast and Pray

Call members to fast and pray for revival on one specific day.

My Kitchen Table

Print stand-up prayer reminder tents for families' dinner tables to encourage families to pray together daily for revival.

Early Morning Prayer

Plan a daily 6:00 a.m. revival prayer time at church.

Lots of Lost Friends

When they committed to pray for lost friends, members at Come As You Are Community Church in Fort Wayne, Indiana, wrote the names of their lost friends on flat eight-inch foam paper dolls. A gigantic Plexiglas box in their sanctuary was filled with them for a visual prayer reminder.

Unique Revival

As long as the purpose is evangelism, your church's evangelistic revival doesn't have to look like last year's. One of the best-attended, most effective revivals our church ever had was a drama revival. The drama evangelist made several trips to our city to teach our church members some evangelistic vignettes. They were amazingly fabulous, and all the actors' friends attended. Many were saved, and God was honored. Get creative. What type of revival might reach the lost in your ministry area? Could you plan a video revival, a music revival, a technorevival?

Baptism on Friday

If it's appropriate at your church, plan a huge baptism service following the last evening's service of your revival.

Revival Planning Teams

Form enthusiastic committees for media, promotion, hospitality, prayer, and a separate team for each night's emphasis. Involve dozens of new and longtime members of all ages as greeters, ushers, counselors, evangelist hosts, choir, band, orchestra, drama, sound, video projection. Place different members in charge of pew signs, flowers, cleanup, child care, food preparation, lights. Engage the whole church to assure that every detail is first-class, "as unto the Lord."

Go Get 'em

Offer free rides from the local nursing home, a well-populated neighborhood, or an apartment complex.

Counselors in Motion

If invitation counselors are seated all around the sanctuary and come forward reverently during the invitation, that movement might make it easier for a lost person to come forward too. If dozens make a decision for Christ, will you have enough counselors?

Mobile Revival

A revival could be mobile. For instance, each service could be scheduled at a different location: the local football stadium, a trailer stage in a store's parking lot, under a tent at the church, at the city park, a ranch, a hilltop, and the last night at the church. Yes, it would take lots of extra effort to publicize and to haul chairs and sound equipment and stages, but imagine how many lost people you might reach.

Simultaneous Revivals

A church could host a revival at the same time as other churches in the area. Ten Baptist churches in Indiana's Northeastern Baptist Association coordinated dates for citywide simultaneous revivals and shared advertising expense.

One-Day Revival

If your church is planning a one-day revival, throw all the effort that would go into a weeklong event.

Bless Your Evangelist

Be a blessing to your evangelist. Send prayer notes. E-pound him with encouragement. Make welcome baskets of local goodies along with a long list of people your church is praying for and inviting to the revival. My pastor/husband blessed many evangelists who stayed at our home by polishing their shoes.

School Beginning

*"The LORD is near all who call out to Him, all who call
out to Him with integrity."*

—Psalms 145:18

It's an important new beginning for students and their parents. Some fresh
ideas to encourage them:

On Sunday

During the Sunday worship service before school begins, invite all school-
teachers, administrators, and personnel from public, private, home-school,
and university to come forward and kneel or stand at the altar. Lead a prayer
of commitment and commissioning, asking God's guidance for these leaders as
they touch the lives of children this year. Commit as a church to pray regularly
for them, and ask God to give them opportunities to show and share his love
with students.

Pray for Students

As an alternative to the idea above, ask all students to come to the altar and
offer a prayer for God's protection and guidance for them during the new
school year.

Moms' Prayer Tea

Advertise this annual event in your local paper to invite all moms to join your
members at the church after they deliver their kids for the first day of school.
Friendly greeters direct ladies to assigned circles for each school, and a facilitator for each group asks moms to introduce themselves and tell their children's
names. The facilitator then prays for each mother and child by name, for school
faculty, and for parents. The prayer time lasts about a half hour with no formal

program—simply a sincere, encouraging time of prayer to dedicate children and schools to God. Play soft Christian music, then raise the music volume to signal closing time. Serve coffee and juice to extend fellowship to those who would like to linger.

Bold Books

Customized paper book covers can be ordered featuring your church and youth group name, events, and Scriptures to encourage students.

Adult Class Project

For the first day of school, a class or church could prepare an enormous, gorgeous basketful of snacks, using a variety of homemade and store-bought sweets and healthy snacks. Deliver the basket to the teachers' lounge of the school nearest your church, along with a note assuring them of your prayers.

Choose a Teacher

Christian teachers who attend your church need your support as they are "on mission" in our community. Challenge members of your church to choose one teacher from your church to pray for and encourage with occasional notes.

Tell a Teacher

Challenge church members to be a strong Christian witness to every teacher who impacts their children. During a school year, they will have numerous opportunities to share Christ, invite teachers to Christian events, and reflect Christ in their actions.

Parking Lot Prayer

Church families could gather in the school parking lot for prayer one day before school begins, then caravan to the local ice cream shop for fellowship.

Student Encouragements

Plan an informal first-day-of-school celebration for high school students. Meet at the church right after school for pizza and a prayer of thanks to God for today's blessings. Alternative: make it a breakfast before school.

First Day of College

Want a high-impact ministry project? Mail homemade cookies and a Scripture verse to every freshman college student in your church, encouraging them to share them as they make new friends.

Scripture of the Year

"I have treasured Your word in my heart."

—Psalms 119:11

Our pastor chose an annual theme Scripture, and the entire church memorized it. It was awesome!

It's Everywhere

The Scripture of the year is prominent in church bulletins, newsletters, stationery, and other printed materials. It's on posters. It's in the library. It's on pencils. It's in Sunday school classrooms. It's on pre-service audiovisuals.

Scripture Banner

Plan ahead for artistic members to create an elaborate banner of the Scripture of the year, and display it prominently all year.

Sing It

A gifted musician in your church may set the Scripture of the year to song.

All Together Now

Lead the congregation to quote the Scripture of the year verse together weekly during worship. Print the words on an audiovisual for guests to read along.

Sidewalk Chalk

On the first Sunday that the annual Scripture of the year is revealed, ask youth to write the Scripture on sidewalks around the church building.

We're First!

Ask a specific children's Sunday school class, i.e. fifth graders, to learn the Scripture of the year before the year begins. They confidently quote the Scripture on the first Sunday of the year to encourage the rest of the congregation to learn it.

On the Fridge

Print the church's Scripture of the year on note cards to put on car visors, dressing mirrors, or school lockers. Create a refrigerator magnet with the Scripture. Repetition will help members memorize the Scripture and apply it in their lives.

Young Artists

Ask elementary-aged Sunday school classes to make a class project involving the Scripture of the year. Each student can write out the verse or illustrate the verse in an artistic way, displaying their art in a prominent hallway one Sunday.

Big and Youthy

Purchase a large piece of canvas or art board to fit a blank wall at the church. An artistic youth or youth team can create a giant masterpiece of the Scripture of the year.

Seminary Students

Invest in future ministers.

"I chose you before I formed you in the womb;
I set you apart before you were born. I appointed
you a prophet to the nations."

—Jeremiah 1:5

God's called them. We'll encourage them. Need fresh ideas to lift up seminary students from your church?

Recognize Them

Encourage the church to pray faithfully for church members who are called to full-time ministry by occasionally printing a list of seminary students in your church newsletter or church bulletin.

Send-Off

Plan a celebration reception after the business meeting when your church votes to endorse a seminary student.

Report

When seminary students are home for holidays, ask them to share testimonies in a Sunday school department, teach a Bible class, or speak at a church event. The pastor may choose to invite the seminary student to preach occasionally.

Still Miss Ya!

As a church, class, or individual, keep in touch with seminary students frequently. Personally write a monthly note, or assign months to several church members. Send care packages. Order pizza delivered during finals. Purchase a

Bible commentary set and send one book monthly. Mail a congratulations card after each semester. Send a singing telegram. Whatever it takes, assure students that their church is praying.

Internship

Invite a seminary student to work in your church as a ministry intern this summer. If a seminary is near your church, strive to create full- or part-time ministry positions for students. The church will be blessed, the student will benefit, and God's kingdom will be impacted. Our church's members who attended seminary had a standing invitation to serve as summer interns.

Scholarships and Gifts

Students preparing for ministry are worthy of your generous investment. Offer to help with a book purchase for a seminary student, or establish one-time or ongoing scholarships through the seminary financial aid office. Consider assisting with funding for the seminary student to attend a Christian conference or an overseas mission trip.

"Adopt" an International Seminary Student

Ask the nearest seminary for the name of a ministerial student from another country, and then develop a supportive friendship.

First Pastorate Shower

A graduating seminary student, who grew up in your church, has accepted his first full-time pastorate. Give him a book shower! Every young minister needs commentaries, Bible dictionaries, Christian magazine subscriptions, current Christian books, and other resources.

Inform

Use seminary bulletin inserts to inform your church about the important ministry of your denomination's seminaries.

Dear Mr. President

If your pastor or ministry staff attended seminary, write that seminary president to tell how your church has benefited and to express your appreciation.

Recognize Their Calling and Commitment

Students complete a four-year college degree before seminary, and then the MDiv seminary degree requires an additional three years of challenging graduate level courses. Seminary is hard work. One of the greatest blessings that God can give a church is to call its members into vocational ministry. Invest in them!

Senior Adults

*"They will still bear fruit in old age, healthy and green,
to declare: "The LORD is just; He is my rock.""*

—Psalm 92:14–15

They're setting the example for the younger generation. Some fresh ideas for seniors:

The Joy Club

Give your church's senior adult group a name. Be creative and choose a name that honors God and fits your church. How about the EB Club (eternal benefits)? The senior adult group at Calvary Baptist, Madison, Indiana, is called DUO (Do unto others).

Bluebonnet Walk

Dallas Baptist University plans an annual bluebonnet walk and hymn singing for senior adults. If the area near your church property has natural beauty, schedule an event to enjoy God's creation.

Shut-in Sing-Along

The senior adult group can schedule ahead to visit homebound members or a local nursing home for a hymn sing-along.

Mission Trip

Plan an annual mission trip for senior adults only. Teach English culture lessons in Germany. Form a kitchen band and perform in Mexico. Help build a church in Russia or Rhode Island.

Ministry Teams

Consider how senior adults in your church will be involved in ministry. Form ministry teams for hospital visitation, school mentoring, welcoming new residents in your community, or church outreach.

Age Doesn't Mean Saved

Remember: just because people are older doesn't mean they're Christians! Always share God's plan of salvation at senior adult events.

Secret Grandma

Our church's fifth graders loved their "secret grandparent" ministry project. Each student was assigned a senior adult and given tips about his or her interests, hobbies, and background. The kids wrote notes, delivered small treats to their doors, left notes in the senior adult Sunday school room, and eagerly anticipated unveiling their identity. They mailed invitations and planned a nice tea where they revealed their identity. Each student had a list of questions to ask senior adults about their life and faith in Christ. They sat by their "secret grandparent" that morning in worship.

Day Trips

Plan exciting senior adult outings as an outreach ministry to seniors in your community. Seniors invite their unchurched friends to come along for a fun outing with their Christian friends, intentionally sharing Jesus as they go.

Cherry Blossom Trip

Many senior adults in your area would enjoy a pleasure trip to a nearby destination. Carefully plan the trip, and incorporate a Bible study or devotional each day. Challenge the group to spend time alone with God daily, and share testimonies of His blessings.

The Next Generation

Seniors can be invaluable during Vacation Bible School by serving snacks, manning crosswalks, and teaching classes. Many children have no grandparents nearby, so they'll treasure time with older adults.

Single Adults

*"An unmarried man . . . or woman . . . is concerned
about the things of the Lord."*

—1 Corinthians 3:32–34

About 40 percent of adults in your city are unmarried. Does your church reflect that statistic?

Quality Leadership

From the beginning stages of your church's singles ministry, seek out the most personable, quality singles for your leadership team. Challenge leadership team members to model Christian values and to attend Sunday Bible study every week.

Vital Church Participation

Encourage singles to be plugged in to worship services, church activities, and church ministries. Single adults need to be vitally involved in church committees, in music ministry, etc. Singles ministry is not parachurch. It is the church!

Quality, Quality, Quality

Background music plays during fellowship time. Registration is efficient. Greeters are well-groomed and friendly. The walls are freshly painted. The décor is tasteful and personal. The Bible teacher is prepared and enthused about God's Word. The Bible study applies to their lives. Ministry projects are visible. Guests are invited to sit with members in worship and to attend a weekday gathering. Class begins and ends on time. And attenders see love for a holy God in action. Every single detail of a Bible class or fellowship must reflect a love for the God you're celebrating.

Koinonia

Name that class! Allow the leadership team to choose a name for the class. It helps with publicity, allows age divisions without stating ages, and conveys class personality. For example, one singles class at our church chose the name Koinonia, which means "Christian fellowship" in Greek.

Fellowship Matters

It's difficult to offer too many fellowship opportunities for single adults. Our group planned large quarterly events, quality monthly events, and multiple smaller gatherings. They met at a coffee shop on Thursdays, planned theater outings, volleyball tournaments, game nights, prayer groups, weeknight Bible studies, holiday get-togethers, ski trips, banquets, whirly-ball games, retreats, a bowling team, and Sunday lunch outings. They loved being together.

Target

Aim at nothing; hit nothing. The most effective way to reach unchurched single adults is to target a specific age group, need, or interest. For example, a class designed for singles, ages twenty-two to thirty-two, will be much more effective than a class for all single adults. A realistic beginning division might be three classes—twenties, thirties and forties, and fifties and up. Additional classes could multiply from those. Some churches offer classes for single parents, divorced singles, widows and widowers, single women, etc.

Fellowship Reaches the Lost

Every major fellowship event should be planned with lost people in mind. Our singles' most successful outreach strategy was a coed softball team in a city league. Friends were invited to play on the team, and large groups attended as spectators. Everyone went out for sodas after games, and every guest was invited to Bible class.

Baptism

When single adults accepted Christ as their Savior, the entire group attended the baptismal service. When the pastor invited friends to stand during the baptism, the entire group joyfully stood up for the new Christian.

Ministry Projects

Help develop the outward focus of your singles group by planning monthly mission projects. Singles in our group loved our missions projects as much as the fellowships! Examples: plan benevolence closet work day, paint the church's mission house, take a shift on the church's live nativity scene, make military care packages, park outreach party, build a porch for a senior adult, design props for church pageants. You get the idea.

Ministering to Members

The biblical command to "love one another" must be taken seriously. When a class member's parent dies, our class makes phone calls, serves dinner, and supports her through those days. When one lost a job, class members circulated her résumé.

Mission Trips

Work with the church missions committee to plan an annual mission trip for singles. Whether it's disaster relief in a neighboring state or helping a missionary in the Bahamas, you'll be amazed at how God can help unify, focus, and grow your group.

Conferences

Take a group of leaders or class members to quality events planned specifically for single adults. LifeWay Glorieta and Ridgecrest Conference Centers provide leader training and a singles conference annually. Attend national and statewide Christian conferences, retreats, and concerts.

Visual Counts

Work hard to create an enticing environment for Bible classes. The classroom must not only be freshly painted and clean; it must be personal and ever changing. Use photos of fellowships, ministry projects, and mission trips. Display Bible-learning visuals. Feature photographs and information about singles who teach in other Bible classes (see Members in Service on page 97).

The Bible Lesson

Enthusiastic, life-changing Bible study is what it's all about! One enemy to quality teaching is sameness. Vary teaching methods to relay the Word of God. Use audiovisuals. Encourage discussion. Apply Scripture to each person's life.

Web Site

Design a Web page for each age division, and link it to the church Web site.

Multiplication DNA

Since singles encompass almost half of adults in your town, one or two singles classes is much too small a goal! You are not forming a private club. You are strategizing to reach hundreds of single adults with the gospel. From the beginning, make multiplication an annual goal of every class. Always have an intern teacher for each class. Set a specific date for multiplication of the class. The only time our singles ministry began to decline was when we decided not to multiply. It's scriptural!

Let's Do Lunch

Our single adult Bible class went out to lunch each Sunday after worship. Guests were invited, and the fellowship was warm. It was a great outreach strategy.

Name Tags Are Necessary

Gotta have name tags. Every person. Every Sunday. Every fellowship. Name tags help members and guests learn names and develop friends.

Registration Desk

Critical! The registration process must be fast, meticulous and comfortable. Use a computer spreadsheet to make a sign-in sheet integrating guests' and members' names, with a * designating guests.

Join Us?

Greeters at the registration table invite guests to join the class. Joining a Bible class should be simple, and it often opens the door for leading a person to Christ and to joining the church.

Involvement

As newcomers join your class, share the responsibilities. Newcomers can greet, make coffee, create a Web site, or plan a retreat or fellowship event. Allow every member to be involved.

Ushers

When our single adult ministry was beginning a new age-division class, our single adults served as ushers during worship for one Sunday. A listing of church activities for single adults was in that morning's bulletin, and church members were able to see our quality singles in action. And some of those singles became regular church ushers.

I Know a Single Adult

Distribute business cards with the singles group meeting time and location, and ask every church member to give it as an invitation to their single friends. When beginning a new age-group division, ask all church members to help with inviting single friends in that age group.

Annual Event

Plan one or two first-class annual events for all singles. Schedule it months in advance, and plan every detail "as unto the Lord"! Give it a great name and advertise it as a citywide singles event. As classes multiply, they'll still enjoy fellowship with one another at the annual events.

Plan Ahead

Single adults are busy people. Every mission trip, fellowship, or mission project should be planned ahead, and dates should be communicated well ahead of time. Publish a monthly calendar and list of upcoming dates.

The List

Our class's fellowship was greatly enhanced because of our class e-mail list. The list was reprinted weekly, and was available at the class registration desk. Guest's names were marked with an asterisk. We sent weekly e-updates, and class members forwarded them to other single friends. (See E-mail section on page 63 for more suggestions.)

Motivating Leaders

Go to www.census.gov to discover proof that almost half of adults in your area are unmarried. Numbers are shown for never-married, widowed, and divorced adults. Display those specific numbers at your leadership meetings. What a mission field!

Sports Evangelism

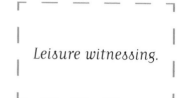

"The training of the body has a limited benefit, but godliness is beneficial in every way."

—1 Timothy 4:8

Isn't it amazing that our great God can use something as simple as a ball to enhance Christian fellowship and open doors to save souls?

Which Sport?

Discover the interests of members in your church, and fit your sports evangelism to those. Possibilities are endless. How about groups for skeet shooting, ultimate Frisbee, three-on-three basketball, table tennis, volleyball, bowling, broomball, fishing, kite flying, cycling, hiking, flag football, Rollerblading, indoor soccer, outdoor soccer, walking, snow skiing, golfing, or softball.

Register Online

If at all possible, allow online registration for sports teams and events.

Ski Trip Tip

Planning a snow ski trip? Purchase brightly colored armbands or ribbon for all skiers to wear the first day of skiing. Fellowship multiplies as skiers learn to recognize one another. After the trip, plan a reunion party with a snow theme. Each skier brings a dish of food, but it must be white. Make notes during the ski trip about funny events, and create an award certificate for each skier. For example, give awards for most improved, best crash, or most unique style.

Golf Tournament

Our annual church golf tournament was a blast. And it was evangelistic. Many businessmen or sports enthusiasts who would never attend church may gladly come for a well-planned church golf tournament. Plan ahead, advertise well, and plan a quality event. Invite every golfer to your church on Sunday, when you will show a group golf photo on the preservice audiovisual.

No Gymnasium Required

A church gym or ball field isn't required to share Christ through sports. Rent a city field. Join a municipal league. Meet at the high school or park. When we planted a church, our members met at a school gym weekly for basketball. Friends brought friends. Christ was shared. Eternity was impacted.

Church Gyms Aren't Made to Sit Vacant

Offer your workout room or gym to local firefighters or police for their officers' use. Designate open hours for walkers and publicize it in the community. Encourage church members to work out regularly and share a witness with guests. Make your gym "the place" to hang out after high school. Your youth minister and members can play a game of basketball and share Jesus! Plan volleyball tournaments or three-on-three basketball tournaments for singles, teens, or couples on Fridays. Advertise a father-daughter basketball or volleyball tournament.

Witnessing Gymnasium Walls

Display Christian art or banners with athletic-type Scriptures (i.e., 1 Tim. 4:8). Display tracts near the entrance, with church event information and witness tracts. Murals around a walking track could explain the plan of salvation.

Count Those Steps

Walkers in the community are welcome to use the gym at Hanover Baptist Church in Indiana. Walkers track their miles walked, and when they reach one hundred miles, they receive a Hanover Baptist Walking/Jogging Club T-shirt.

Roll 'em In

Many churches purchase skates and open their gym for community-wide skate nights. Play Christian music, have fun games and prizes, and invite families to come back for worship on Sunday.

Aerobics as Ministry

An exercise class can be a great church fellowship and community outreach. Exercise to Christian music. The instructor should be a member of your church and may conclude or begin each class with a Scripture reading.

Wheelchair Aerobics

Consider offering exercise classes specifically geared toward special groups, such as senior adults, moms and preschoolers, or people in wheelchairs. Gather a base group of participants from your church, then advertise the class to the local community. The key, of course, is an enthusiastic and prepared instructor. A well-attended, low-impact exercise class for senior adults in our church simply met in a classroom and exercised to Christian music at their chairs.

Leagues and Tournaments

Form teams or tournaments for men, women, teens, or children. Even better, target specific groups, i.e. high school coed team, men over forty, college students, third and fourth graders, or thirty-something singles. Children's sports leagues, such as Upward Basketball or Sunshine Soccer, can provide an enormous opportunity to reach young families in your community.

Smile When You Dribble

Non-Christians must observe the joy that we have in Jesus! Good sportsmanship is an absolute necessity for Christian sports. Fellowship is essential. Go out for Cokes after the game. Let guests see Christian joy in action.

First Baptist Jerseys

Print great-looking team shirts, and be sure the church name is on it. Put your church's name on trophies, name tags, award certificates, registration forms, team photograph, bowling shirts, team jerseys, etc. Hang a church banner on the dugout. Let the spectators and opponent team know who you represent.

Thank God

Have a team prayer before and after the church team's game.

Devotional at Half-Time

Offer a dynamic two-minute devotional at halftime for your church's sports teams.

Hey You!

When guests join your team, make a point to learn their names right away. Open your circle of friendship and include them immediately.

See Ya Sunday

At the end of the game, distribute printed invitations to spectators to come to Sunday worship, Bible study, Vacation Bible School, or a special church event.

Will the Fighting Squirrels Please Stand?

Invite the team to sit together during worship one Sunday.

Let's Go for Soda

Invite guests on the team to join the group for after-game snacks.

Better Than Baseball

Actively witness on and off the field to team members who don't know Christ as their Savior. Talk about God. Just being a good sport or a nice guy won't save anyone! Tell teammates how Jesus has changed your life.

Meet Brother Bob

Invite the pastor to a game and introduce him to newcomers.

Cool Socks, Dude

Make it fun. Your church team can really stand out by wearing matching hair ribbons, armbands, or jerseys. One of our softball teams actually wore red striped tube socks one season, wild ties another year, and green golf pants another. I'm not really advocating that, but they really livened up that league!

Come Watch Us Lose on Tuesday

List time and location for church sports team games in the church bulletin.

Hurry! Find a Guest

To encourage outreach, some teams require a certain number of nonchurch members on each roster. Advertise in the local newspaper during registration.

Season Finale

Planning a big end-of-season celebration can create a great witness opportunity. Throw a great party for the team and their families, present trophies or fun award certificates, and show slides or video of the season. Then have your pastor or coach or a respected team member share his testimony and briefly, but sincerely and enthusiastically, share the gospel.

Sunday Night Ideas

Can't wait for Sunday
night church!

"Zeal for Your house will consume me."

—John 2:17

Need fresh ideas for your church's Sunday evening worship service? With planning, every service can be unique. A few ideas:

Baptism or Lord's Supper Service

A monthly Sunday evening worship service can be planned exclusively around baptisms. It can be the highlight of every month! Our church observed the Lord's Supper four times each year. Two of those were Sunday mornings, and two entire Sunday evening services were dedicated to observance of the ordinance.

Sunday Night Electives

A series of Sunday evening services could begin with great Christian music, then offer a choice of discipleship electives.

Everybody Praise

Invite each choir in your church to plan an entire evening of music or musical drama for Sunday night church annually. No senior choir or youth choir at your church? No problem! Form one just for a special evening service.

A "Sanging"

Enjoy an entire worship service of congregational praise. Add variety with song requests, instrumental diversity, antiphonal singing, a cappella music, and style diversity.

Hanging of the Greens

The Sunday evening service after Thanksgiving can be planned as a Hanging of the Greens service, a joyful time of adorning God's house for Christmas.

Mission Fair

The church's annual mission fair can occur on a Sunday night. (See Mission's Fair for ideas.)

Sunday Night Vacation Bible School

Some churches spread out Vacation Bible School over five consecutive Sunday evenings, planning quality classes for children, as well as adults and teens.

Christian Concert

Bring friends to hear guest musicians in concert.

College Night at Christmas

Members of your church who are home from university for Christmas break can plan the entire evening service, sharing music, drama, and testimonies of how God is at work in their lives.

Vacation Bible School Family Night

The Sunday evening before Vacation Bible School may be dedicated to prayer for leaders and children who will attend. The Sunday evening after VBS could be used as a "show and tell" type service, allowing children to quote Scriptures or sing songs or otherwise relate what they've learned during the week.

Mission Trip Report

When a group from your church returns from a mission trip, invite them to plan an entire Sunday evening service to report their stories.

Youth Camp

One of my favorite services of the year was the Sunday evening after youth camp. Teens sang and gave testimonies of how God impacted their lives. Those who gave their hearts to Christ during camp were baptized, and the entire church got to see the results of a great ministry.

Missionary Speaker

If a furloughing missionary shares a testimony during morning worship, church members will look forward to an entire evening service led by the missionary.

Take Five Revival

Schedule five inspiring guest speakers to speak for five consecutive Sunday evening services.

20–20–20

At Northwoods Baptist in Indiana, Pastor Bobby Pell plans a monthly 20–20–20 service. The first twenty minutes is Bible study, the next twenty is discussion, and the last twenty is music. A big timer is set, and when it dings, the next phase begins. Simple. But the church loves it. And they dismiss on time.

My Question's Important

Pastor Kevin Bryant at Southwood Baptist Church in Beech Grove, Indiana, plans several "Bible forums" each year. For weeks ahead church members are encouraged to submit questions about the Bible and the pastor dedicates an entire evening service to giving biblical answers to questions about everything from dinosaurs to predestination.

Training Events

A Sunday evening can be set aside for discipleship training classes.

Summer Nights

Plan a series of several Sunday evening programs during the summer, and advertise them as a "summer nights" series. The worship services could be Christian drama, music, topical, or educational.

Another Sunday Worship

Some churches plan an alternative worship service or a second or third worship service for a targeted group of people, such as singles or people who cannot attend on Sunday mornings.

Ready and Waiting

Plan an annual evangelism training event on a Sunday evening. Offer multiple choices of classes about how to witness, such as witnessing with a marked New Testament, relationship witnessing, salvation bracelets, etc.

Dramatic Evening

Your church drama team or a guest dramatic group from a nearby university or church can present Christian sketches or a full-hour drama.

Deacon Ordination

When new deacons are selected, consider planning a Sunday evening service for deacon ordination.

Sunday School/ Small Groups

If your class
isn't growing and
multiplying, maybe it's
time to make a plan!

"They welcomed the message with eagerness and examined the Scriptures daily to see if these things were so. Consequently, many of them believed."

—Acts 17:11–12

It's where newcomers get discipled and find friends. Some fresh ideas:

Am I Late?

It's one of the best indicators of a growing class: lots of early arrivers! Class leaders and greeters must arrive well before the first class member to turn on the lights, crank up the coffeepot, start a music CD, and set a joyful mood.

A Simple "Freshen-Up"

Rearrange your classroom regularly. Change the direction chairs face. Use semicircles instead of rows. Put chairs in groupings of threes for a discussion starter. Or place chairs around tables for a change. Add a stool for the teacher. Make simple, insignificant changes in arrangement.

Secret Ingredients

Two important elements of a successful, effective Bible class: joy and (surprise!) quality, life-changing Bible study. Structure class time so that nothing else takes priority over getting into God's Word! And enjoy serving. God once remanded his people, "Because you didn't serve the LORD your God with joy and a cheerful heart, even though you had an abundance of everything" (Deut. 28:47).

An Empty Chair

If all chairs are taken when guests arrive at your Bible class, they do not feel welcomed. Always have extra chairs set up and ready for guests.

Hi Shirley

Create permanent name tags for class members, using a large font that is readable from several feet away. Name tags improve fellowship, promote accountability, and help new members quickly feel that they belong.

Reprint Class Contact List Often

Really often. A guest or new member should be asked if they would mind having their name on the class list next week. Then print a new list *before they return!* This simple act says, "You're accepted." Print an asterisk by names of guests on the list and encourage them to join the class when they're ready.

Growth Chart

Keep a Sunday school growth chart on the back of your classroom door. Use a computer to create simple visual charts of Sunday school class attendance. By adding weekly attendance, the chart can be printed weekly. It's an effective, easy way to see if your class is stagnant or growing.

Fellowship or Flounder

Wonder why your quality Bible class is not growing as you'd like? Try adding predictable, consistent Christian fellowship. Some growing classes eat lunch together every Sunday after church. Some sit together in worship. Others plan quarterly fellowship events. Our singles' class met Tuesdays for prayer, Thursdays at the coffee shop, and Fridays for a bowling league. *Then* they planned trips, mission projects, and fellowship events! What's great for one group may be overkill for another, but every class needs fellowship opportunities.

Let's Go!

Plan purposeful travel for class members. Take leaders to Glorieta or Ridgecrest or another quality training conference. Go together to a women's retreat or men's conference. A Friday evening family camping trip, a professional ball game, a bike trip, or a day on the lake. Schedule well ahead of time, plan well, and enjoy getting to know class members. Important: be back for Sunday's class. Guests will be there!

My Aunt Sally's Neighbor's Niece

Praying for one another is vital. During Sunday morning Bible study, however, prayer request time must not overtake Bible study. If your class spends too much time listing people who are sick, consider gathering written prayer requests and making copies to distribute.

Move It!

If your church's Sunday school is growing, it will most likely be necessary to relocate class meeting rooms to accommodate growth. It's healthy to change classrooms occasionally. Side benefits: moving to a new classroom creates a new energy and freshness. It gives a reason to contact former members. It makes you clean your classroom. So paint, clean, and personalize your classroom as your church allows, but always be ready joyfully to relocate when asked!

Begin Which New Classes?

To reach new people for Christ, it is imperative to start new Bible classes. Need ideas? Single adults, divided by decades. Ladies class. Men's class. Middle-aged couples class. Businessmen's class. Policemen's class. Younger adult class, multiplied from your present young adult class. New children's age division. Nearly-wed class for engaged couples. New parents class. A new class list of inactive members. Begin planning today for new Bible classes.

Singles, Age 22–32

Our church had strong, quality singles Bible studies, but almost every attender was over the age of thirty. We targeted young single adults, age 22 to 32 for a new class. It exploded! For new classes, target specific age groups.

Engaged Couples Class

It was the most successful class in our church for bringing young adults to Bible study. See details in "Wedding/Anniversary" section.

Countdown to New Class Start

Gather a "dream team" of at least three committed people who will pray, plan, set goals, and prepare. Set a class beginning date at least three months away. Enlist a quality Bible teacher. Begin a database of potential attenders. Publicize. Work hard to assure a good attendance on the first day, and begin with a bang!

Stagnate or Multiply

Did your Sunday school class or small group reproduce last year? Build multiplication into the DNA of your class. Make it a goal for every Bible class to multiply at least annually. Talk about it. Plan it. Set a date. Every Bible class needs an intern teacher.

Multiplication Day

Ask every class member to pray about which class they will attend after multiplication. Preplan so the division will be fairly equal in number. On multiplication Sunday the two leaders stand on a different side of the room, and members are asked to divide themselves fairly equally between two sides of the rooms. Recognize the two new classes in worship and celebrate multiplication.

Thanksgiving

> It's not really about the turkey.

> *"I will fervently thank the LORD with my mouth; I will praise Him in the presence of many."*
>
> —Psalm 109:30

Never miss an opportunity to thank your God. Some fresh ideas:

Blessing Baskets

Collect or purchase inexpensive baskets, and give one to each family in your church or class on the first Sunday in November. An instruction sheet requests that they keep the blessing basket on their kitchen table all month. Each day family members write something they're thankful for and put it in the basket. On a designated Sunday before or after Thanksgiving, members bring baskets to worship, sit as a family and bring their baskets to the altar in gratitude to God.

Thankful Parade

During the Bible study hour children or youth could make large one-word signs to show things they're thankful for. Attach signs to yardsticks and allow children to march into worship. As they line the aisles with thanksgiving signs, lead the congregation in a prayer of thanksgiving.

Harvest Celebration

If you live in a farming community, you might enjoy this idea I saw at a Ukrainian church. An important annual harvest celebration was planned at the peak of harvest season. Members brought the biggest and best vegetables and produce from their farms and gardens. The worship center was decorated beautifully with a harvest theme, and the produce was used to create a gorgeous centerpiece wagon on the stage. The pastor's message used harvest and thankful themes from Scripture, and all the people gave thanks to God for his abundant blessings. At a fun celebration after worship, the produce was cut into small pieces and served.

God's at Work

Begin on Thanksgiving Sunday for a yearlong weekly tradition. Every Sunday during worship a different church member enthusiastically shares a three-minute testimony about how Jesus is working in their personal life and in their place of ministry in the church. We called it "What's Jesus Doing Now?" The testimonies may be presented as a carefully timed live testimony or, even better, as a videotaped talk.

Vacation Bible School Evangelism

"In the same way, it is not the will of your Father in heaven that one of these little ones perish."

—Matthew 18:14

The Big Question: How can we inspire every church member *personally* to invite an unchurched child they know to Vacation Bible School (VBS)? Here are some fresh ideas that work!

Tickets

Using clip art to simulate an official ticket, print FREE at the top, and give exciting VBS details including dates, times, ages, free snacks, recreation, etc. During Sunday school, give each child tickets to give to their twenty best friends. Of course, they can give more if they desire! Some may want to give tickets to their entire school class, soccer team, or ballet class.

Pop the Question

At the close of worship on Sunday before VBS, announce that each person will receive a helium-filled balloon after church. Attach VBS invitations to each balloon, and commission members personally to deliver that balloon before it deflates to a child they know who doesn't regularly attend church anywhere. You may use preprinted or plain helium-quality balloons, and rent or purchase a helium tank to fill them just before the worship service. Note: It takes a few hours to prepare the balloons.

Just One

Need a tip on how to distribute VBS flyers easily? During Sunday school or worship announcements, ask each person who will hang one VBS flyer in a public place this week to stand. Distribute flyers to them, and they'll cover your city in no time.

E-Invitations

A wonderful, personal, *free* method of advertising is to use e-mail invitations. Design your own or use those provided on the lifeway.com Web site. Ask every child or adult in your church to send one to their entire e-mail address book.

Take It to the Streets

Stage a big biking, jogging, or walking event, asking lots of your church members to meet at a starting point and distribute VBS flyers as they go. Print VBS T-shirts for participants and make signs and banners about VBS. You could even use a professional event service for running and walking events, with starting lines and finish times. Charge a small entry fee and contribute it to missions.

Get Outdoors

Set up a colorful outdoor Vacation Bible School registration party. Plan a bicycle parade down the sidewalks near your church. Deliver invitations to kids in the neighborhood or at a local park.

Drive-By Enticement

Our hundred-year-old downtown church once rented a thirty-foot gorilla balloon to hold a VBS sign on top of our building. Our record number of first-time guests at VBS certainly was a result of the ape! Consider renting "dancing tube guys" to attract attention to your outdoor banner. Use the VBS theme to spur ideas for outdoor advertising interest, i.e. a flamingo flock. Important fact: to make VBS evangelistic, you have to invite lost people to attend.

Invitation in the Sky

How about a kids' kite-flying day or fishing contest? Stake your VBS banner nearby, and offer early registration during the event. Be sure to fly one VBS-theme kite. Make it a special day by awarding trophies for biggest and littlest fish, highest, fanciest, and longest-flying kites.

Use All Available Media

Explore the use of cable TV's free community ads, flyers, posters, radio, billboards, newspaper ads or inserts, and theater ads. Print grocery-bag inserts.

Use the exterior sign at church. Write a short feature story for the local newspaper, and submit it with a captivating photo of workers preparing for VBS. Order yard signs for members' lawns.

Mom, Can I Go?

It costs nothing extra to decorate the hallways and classrooms for Vacation Bible School one week early. VBS leaders can get the entire church into the mood for VBS by decorating early, and the church family will catch the excitement. It will encourage them to pray for VBS and to invite their neighborhood children and friends to attend. Sunday school classes who care about the lost world won't mind the inconvenience, and VBS will be less stressful for workers.

Puppet Invitation

Create a small puppet stage in the corner of a busy church foyer. Use simple sock puppets or elaborate puppets to sing, invite, and tell kids passing by all about VBS.

Just a Minute

Our church wrote one-minute skits to perform during Sunday morning worship for three Sundays before VBS begins. Yes, they were literally one minute, but they made quite an impact!

Roving Roman Road

Pastor Jim Bohrer at Hope Community Church in Brownsburg, Indiana, creates a unique witnessing costume each year and spends his VBS time in the hallways and classrooms with the specific intention of sharing God's plan of salvation. Last summer he was a roving Roman Road construction worker, complete with orange vest and hardhat. Verses from Romans were attached all over his costume, making it fun and simple to share a witness.

Where the Kids Are

Ready to distribute outreach invitations to VBS? Make a list of the top ten places you can find lots of children during summer. Consider ways to impact those sites, and then plan a huge VBS invitation day, sending church members to blitz the community.

Gonna Love it!

Directors and teachers of each class should obtain a complete list of all children enrolled in their age division in Sunday school and every child who has visited the church during the past year for church, sports teams, fall festival, or other events. Divide the list among VBS workers and personally call to invite each child.

alentines

It's a great time to applaud Christian marriages.

"I sleep, but my heart is awake. A sound! My love is knocking!"

—Song of Songs 5:2

Every holiday gives extra opportunities to share Christ. Some fresh ideas:

Valentine's Outreach

Design an attractive heart-themed advertisement for your local paper: "Looking for the perfect Valentine's gift? Bring your sweetheart to church this Sunday! Pastor Hearn's sermon, 'Love For a Lifetime.'" (Use correct name and sermon title, of course.)

PowerPoint Valentines

Does your church use PowerPoint for Sunday announcements? On Sunday before Valentine's Day, intersperse the announcements with photos of couples in your church. Use subtitles like "Doug and Nancy Schultze, married twenty-five years." Get a quote from one spouse that honors God and their loved one, such as, "She's the best gift God ever gave me!"

Heart Candies

Teens could pass out Christian Valentine candies (sold at most Christian book-stores) at the exits after worship.

Couples Night Out

Provide child care on Valentine's evening for married couples in your church. Make it a Valentine's party for the children, creating a "daddy loves mommy" craft and serving heart snacks.

Sunday School Class Opener

In a married couples Bible class, ask husbands to tell, in ten words or less, why they fell in love with their wife. Ask each wife to face her husband and quietly tell him two things she most admires about him.

Romantic Banquet

Plan an unforgettable dinner for the married couples in your Bible class or church. Create a "Tunnel of Love" theme using Christmas lights and candlelight. Take couple photos as they arrive and have them printed as a memento before they leave. Volunteer waiters wear black and white or tuxedos, drape a towel over their arm, and have eyebrow-pencil-painted curly mustaches. A strolling guitarist or violinist provides love music during a four-course meal, and a Christian comedian talks about love.

Wedding Vow Renewal Ceremony

Plan a special afternoon service for all members, young and old, who would like to renew their wedding vows. Use wedding decorations, and invite relatives and friends. Couples all stand at the altar as the pastor leads the vow renewal. Conclude the ceremony with a lovely reception, complete with a giant wedding cake.

W̶eb S̶ite

I have become all things to all people, so that I may by all means save some.

—1 Corinthians 9:22

Build or expand this amazing outreach tool. Some fresh ideas:

Get a Web Site!

When I began looking for a church in my new town, I didn't check the phone book or call the Baptist state office. Before I even arrived in town, I looked on the Internet. Lost people will do that. Even a simple presence on the Web will make a difference. Get a Web site!

Indiana Pastor Greg Byman says it well:

> We believe any church who is serious about engaging our culture with the gospel must maintain a web presence that is excellent and up-to-date. It's one more door into the church. Or at least a window for seekers to peer in.

445 Visitors Last Month

Did your church have 445 visitors last month? Come As You Are Baptist, Fort Wayne, Indiana, did—on their Web site! They are 445 souls who could potentially become an eternal part of God's family! Add a counter to your site to actually count the number of times someone looks at your site.

Any Size Church

Every size church can have a quality Web site! Professional Web designers are increasingly affordable. Many church Web sites are designed by church members—from teenagers to Web-savvy elderly members. A young teen at a small church recently designed a top-quality site for his church, and he'd never had a Web design class. Just do it!

Quick Click

Your church Web site should answer these questions with one click or less: What time does worship begin? What do you offer my children? How do I get to the church? What should I wear? Who is welcome? Why should I come this Sunday? What is a telephone and e-mail contact?

Tips for Your First Visit

Your church Web site can have a section that offers a few tips for a first-guest. Give outsiders a clue about where to park and how long the worship service will last. They'll be more comfortable coming inside if they're read that there is a welcome kiosk just inside the door. Tell them what's offered for children and the types of classes offered for adults. Many will wonder what to wear. Make them comfortable by telling them what to expect.

Doctrinal Beliefs

A church Web site should give a statement of doctrinal beliefs to help potential attenders understand your church values.

Photo Album

A picture really is worth a thousand words. Use lots of photographs on your church Web site. Photos should reflect the joy of Christ, various ages and ethnicities of your church membership, and lots of activity shots.

Youth Page/Kids Page

If your church has a variety of youth or children's activities, create a page for your Web site to feature them.

Bible Classes or Small Groups

List Bible study classes or small groups and their age divisions or groupings on your church Web site. Print times and meeting place. A photo of the teacher or class would make it even more inviting.

Upcoming Sermon Series

Is your pastor preaching a sermon series? Highlight it on the church Web site. If he uses outlines or schedules topics ahead of time, print upcoming topics.

The Way to Heaven

Never miss an opportunity to share God's plan of salvation. A church Web site can clearly and simply share the gospel, offering a way to respond online, by mail, or by telephone.

Church Tour

A virtual tour of the church is interesting for a guest to your church Web site. A church that is building a new building could post floor plans and photos of progress.

Free Gift

Prepare a small gift to deliver to the home of anyone who requests it online. Use the contact information for Bible study invitation and church contact.

Video Testimony

A short video of a church member's view of your church can be quite effective on your Web site. If your church is doing weekly "What's Jesus Doing Now" testimonies (see "Thanksgiving" section), put those on the Web site.

Last Week's Sermon

What a great way to entice Web-surfers to come to your church! Make your pastor's sermons available on the church Web site for online listening.

Video of Worship Service

If possible, provide a video of a worship service at your church. Audio is good; video is better. A Web-surfer could see a baptism firsthand, hear the pastor's sermon, watch worshippers joyfully singing, and feel more comfortable about attending worship there.

Coming This Sunday

Display current information about the church by printing the church newsletter or a listing of upcoming events. A visitor to your Web site should be able to know what's happening.

Weekly Scripture Verse

Some church Web sites offer a weekly Scripture or devotional from Scripture.

Submit Prayer Requests

A Web site can provide a simple form for visitors to the site to request specific prayer.

Questionnaire

A "Tell Me More" response form on the church Web site can create interest and obtain contact information for Web visitors.

Online Event Registration

Allow visitors to your Web site to register for Bible studies, luncheons, retreats, recreation teams, and Vacation Bible School. This can be one of the most effective uses of a Web site.

How to Join

Attempt to answer questions on your church Web site before they're asked. Give specifics about requirements to join your church. Let visitors know they are welcome.

Who's the Pastor?

Guests to your church Web site will enjoy seeing a photo and reading testimony and resume for your pastor and other church staff members.

Bible Teachers, Deacons, and Other Leaders

Photographs and lists of church leadership on the church Web site can offer a great insight into your church's strong points.

E-Invitation

Want to make it simple for church members to invite their friends? Design several versions of e-invitations for them to forward to their address book or a specific friend.

Ask the Pastor

Our church Web site featured an "Ask the Pastor" site where children could submit a question about Christianity or the Bible and receive an answer from the pastor.

Last Week at Our Church

By placing event photos from last week on your church Web site, visitors will catch the flavor of what's happening. If your church recently presented a great musical or event, place a video of it online.

Wanna Come Back?

Create a click to make your church Web site a Web surfer's home page.

Library Page

List new and recommended reading available in your church library. Book reviews and research links would also be helpful.

Church History

Offer a brief history of the church on the Web site, including links to denominational pages.

Where Is This Church?

Print a map of the church location on your church Web site, along with printed directions from different directions.

Denominational Links

For example, if your church is Southern Baptist, create links on your church Web site to the Southern Baptist Convention, the North American Mission Board, the International Mission Board, your state convention, your local association, LifeWay Christian Resources, Baptist Press, Women on Mission, etc.

More Links

You may further wish to link to community Web sites, movie reviews, Christian music link, and other carefully selected sites of interest to guests to your church Web page.

Right Now

If someone is searching the Internet for a church in your town, can they peer into your church?

Weddings and Anniversaries

Let your fountain be blessed, and take pleasure
in the wife of your youth.

—**Proverbs 5:18**

Celebrate special life moments. Some fresh ideas:

Candelabras and Arches

If it's possible for your church to purchase candleholders or wedding archways for use by those married there, it's a good investment. Make them available to wedding parties for a small donation or free of charge.

Christian Wedding Banner

The banner team at our church created a gorgeous wedding banner to fit a particular sermon, but it was used by dozens of brides as part of their wedding decoration.

Nearly-wed Class

Create a ten-week "It Takes Three" Seminar for couples engaged to be married. A director organizes ten self-contained, interactive, topical Bible classes with different church members leading each class. For example, a Christian CPA in our church taught a class about finances, providing Scriptures and biblical answers as well as budgeting tips and forms. Each instructor uses multiple teaching methods and distributes handouts. We charged a fee for the seminar to cover the cost of a class notebook, a book about Christian marriage, and certificates. Couples were expected to view a video of any class they missed.

One class period was planned together with the youngest married couples class in the church, familiarizing nearly-weds with the joy of weekly Bible study as a couple. Couples were recognized in worship and presented a certificate after completion of the seminar and were invited to join the young married Bible class, even if their wedding was a few weeks later. Weekly sessions had catchy titles, and couples anticipated each topic. Topic possibilities include: finances, intimacy, roles, communication, longevity of marriage, spiritual growth, parenting, in-laws, expectations, conflict, God's plan for marriage, etc. Invite engaged couples from your community to join those from your church. Plan a booth at the local bridal show for outreach registration for the class. Place an invitation in the community events section of your local paper. Watch engagement announcements in the local newspaper, and use Internet reverse directories to find an address to mail an invitation to the class. Our church scheduled a nearly-wed seminar twice each year, and the response was overwhelming.

Fiftieth Wedding Anniversaries

As an annual celebration take a few minutes during worship one Sunday each March to recognize all couples in the church who will celebrate their fiftieth wedding anniversary during that year. Thank God for Christian marriage. Use their current photo and a wedding photo to create a lovely display or audiovisual presentation. In our church the pastor introduces each couple, presents flowers and certificates, and reads a short quotation from them answering this question: "What's the key to making marriage last?" Younger couples want to know! And God will be honored.

Instant Anniversary Party

One Sunday school class in our church worked to gather beautiful reception decorations for twenty-fifth and fiftieth wedding anniversary parties. Everyone in the church was encouraged to borrow them for their anniversary celebration. The collection included lace tablecloths, silver and gold lame fabrics, and an archway with ivy and flowers. The anniversary kit held several lovely "Happy 50th (and 25th) Anniversary" signs, exterior directional signs for guests, and gold and silver helium balloons purchased in bulk. There was a file of punch recipes, tips for planning a gold or silver anniversary, and photos of decoration ideas from past parties. Our church had punch and coffee service and glass plates and utensils for a crowd, so planning a lovely celebration was simple and inexpensive. Occasionally, a party-giver would donate a small monetary gift to help add new items.

Women's Ministry

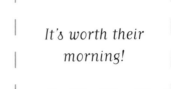

It's worth their morning!

> *"But with good works, as is proper for women who affirm that they worship God."*
>
> —1 Timothy 2:10

A quality women's program can help grow a church. Here are a few tips.

Name It

Some churches enjoy giving their women's ministry a unique name. Our ladies' ministry was called LIGHT, an acronym for Ladies Intentionally Going, Helping, Touching. Choose a clever and inviting name that describes your group's purposes. It's much more enticing to invite a friend to LIGHT than to "our regular weekly women's group."

Leadership Team

Our women's leadership team included the coordinator for each area of our women's ministry—ministry team coordinator, Bible and crafts classes coordinator, luncheon coordinator, Women on Mission coordinator, publicity coordinator, and overall women's ministry coordinator. Always include the pastor's wife as an exofficio member of the team, valuing her input and involvement.

All Together Now

If your church has several small pieces of women's ministries, such as a Bible study, mission group, or craft class, consider pulling them all together on the same day of the week. Publicity can be more effective. Child care can be more accessible. And all the groups will benefit from the energy of a large group.

When our church put all our small groups on the same day, every group grew and flourished, joyfully serving the same God and working together to reach women for Christ.

The Kickoff

An annual women's ministry kickoff event can draw crowds of women. It should be a fabulous annual event where ladies can register for all the women's ministries offered through your church.

Planning Day

Our women's leadership team scheduled one all-day planning meeting each spring to plan for the following year. We began by reviewing evaluations from the current year and used the church, school, and community calendar to schedule for the next fall and spring.

Annual Calendar

It's an important necessity. Plan the church women's program for an entire year. Include retreats, annual or seasonal events, and weekly or monthly classes or ministry teams. Reveal the annual calendar at a kickoff event. This calendar brochure can be used all year for newcomers and guests.

Date Magnet

Create a year's listing of women's regular and special events on a small laminated card. Add a magnet on the back, and distribute the schedule to every woman in the church. When Sally's new neighbor comes for coffee, she can glance at the schedule and invite her to the May luncheon.

Lime Green Paper

Each year select a unique paper color for your women's group. For example, one year's color could be hot pink; another might be pastel orange. Print every woman's ministry program, handout, advertisement, or letter on that paper. Use it for missionary birthday prayers, for poster trim colors, for the kickoff event's color scheme. You'll be surprised at how effectively this color method aids marketing.

Logo for Ladies

Ask an artistic member to create a logo for your women's ministry group, and include it on all publicity. Quality promotional pieces help promise a quality event.

Just Add Flowers

Simple touches of color, flowers, or seasonal decor demonstrate to attenders that your event is important. Just add flowers.

Missionary Support

No matter what type of women's program your church offers, don't forget to include at least tidbits of missions education. If your church is Southern Baptist, it's exciting for women to learn about the thousands of missionaries your church supports around the world. Distribute missionaries' newsletters. Use the *Missions Mosaic* magazine to find names of every missionary who celebrates a birthday that day, and give each person one prayer assignment name. Occasionally challenge the entire group to send an encouraging e-mail to a specific missionary. Plan an occasional group project to collect needed items to assist with a church mission trip.

The Fellowship Factor

Never forget the importance of friendship and fellowship in your women's ministry. Allow time at every event for informal socializing. Plan something different each year to pair women as prayer partners, mentors or lunch groups. Schedule brown-bag luncheons at the home of leaders. Encouraging fellowship will enhance Christian women's lives and increase attendance.

God's Little Ones (GLO)

Quality child care is an essential element of daytime women's programs at your church. Most of our women's ministry budget went to child care. Simply taking turns in the nursery will discourage many potential attenders and will deplete numbers. Check with a nearby church for possible workers to hire. Give a special name, such as GLO, to the child care portion of your women's ministry. Provide a curriculum with a Bible story and weekly memory verse. Add one special element that occurs exclusively during GLO, such as a story time in the library or a simple puppet show written and performed by older homeschooled children.

Ladies Luncheons

One of the most effective outreach strategies of our church was our quarterly ladies luncheons. They were predictably gorgeous, precisely timed so working women could attend and definitely fun to attend. Tickets were sold so women bought lunch tickets for unchurched friends. Our stated purpose was to offer a quality event for Christian women to bring friends to hear about Christ. The inspirational speaker's topic related specifically to women and always included the plan of salvation. Everyone anxiously awaited the next luncheon because it was fast paced, first-class, and worth attending.

Youth

"Flee from youthful passions, and pursue righteousness, faith, love, and peace."

—2 Timothy 2:22

Mother-Daughter Sleepover

Plan at least one mother-daughter overnight party every year. Lead a short lesson and discussion using a theme; then enjoy fellowship and girly stuff, such as manicures. Theme ideas: princess party (child of the King), pirate theme (finding treasures in heaven), pig theme (Proverbs 11:22 about discretion).

Database

Keep updated database and e-mail group list for all youth, youth by grade, youth workers, parents of youth, and youth leadership team.

Mission Trip

Take the youth in your church on a mission trip to another country. It will change their lives, grow their faith, and impact the world.

Celebrate "Birth" Days

When a teen accepts Christ as Savior, encourage all youth to attend the baptismal service, then throw a party afterward to celebrate.

Front and Center

Choose a location near the front of worship and unofficially designate it the "youth section" for teens to sit together. Ask your student leaders to commit to sit there, and others will follow their example.

Guys-Only Campout

Plan an annual campout for teen boys, and teach basic camping skills. Dads can come too. Students will love spending time with Christian men.

Prime Time for a Big Event

Shortly before school begins, plan a huge event. This is not your big evangelism event of the year. Whether it's a cookout, retreat, party, or mission trip, the purpose of the event should be to bind your core youth and challenge them to live a commited life and impact their campus.

Lunch at School

It doesn't take much time, it's inexpensive, and it's one of the best ways a youth worker can encourage students. Have lunch at your students' school with them! First, check with the school about their rules. Then stop by the school weekly to have lunch with students in your youth group. You'll enjoy important conversations, and many will introduce their friends. If it's allowed, bring in a stack of pizzas or some Rice Krispie treats occasionally. And give one to the secretary.

Passion People

Carefully select a small group of student leaders and unofficially designate them as your "passion team." Their responsibility is to welcome and include visitors, to be vitally involved in worship, and to help involve their friends. Meet with the team occasionally to give them encouragement and tips. The passion team is an unofficial designation, but they take their responsibility seriously.

Church Involvement

Help students discover their gifts and use them in the church. Students can serve as ushers or greeters, as well as be in the church worship team, the praise band, the drama team, and the choir. They can use their artistic abilities, write poetry, do graphic design, offer technical assistance, do Web design, help with organization, and the list can go on and on.

Service Opportunities

Discover needs in your town, and help students find a way to meet them. Whether it's a soup kitchen, prison, homeless shelter, or a program for under-privileged children, students will enjoy serving in His name.

Summer Youth Missionary

If your church cannot have a full-time youth minister, consider a summer youth minister. Involve youth workers so the ministry can continue. Contact a seminary, university, or your state denominational office for résumés.

Start a Youth Service

Plan a regular worship service geared just for teens. Choose a time that fits your church's schedule, such as Wednesday evenings. Music, drama, and teachings should be biblically based and specifically targeted toward youth.

Time to Listen

At the end of Sunday morning or small-group Bible study, leave time for prayer requests and discussion of how God is working in students' lives.

Discipleship

Recruit quality Christian adults in your congregation who would be willing to devote a half hour or hour every week to sitting with one or two students to discuss their daily time with God, encourage their relationship with parents, and help them be accountable in their thought life and their words.

Hard Topics

Don't "dumb down" topics addressed at youth events. Youth face the difficult issues daily and need consistently to hear a biblical view. For example, plan a purity class annually.

E-Invitations

Make computer-generated invitations for regular or special youth events, and ask youth to forward them to their e-mail address books.

No Kids Allowed

Never call your students "kids." Call them "students," "teenagers," "youth." Call them "hey, you," but don't call them "kids!" Not at leaders meetings. Not *to* them, not *about* them, not *ever*. Youth are not little children.

Summertime Fun

- Occasionally plan the weekly summer youth meeting outside at a park (complete with water balloon fight, of course.)
- Plan multiple weekly events during the summer. Have Mystery Monday, Wednesday youth service, Friday night events, etc. Important: each event must be free or inexpensive.

- Take advantage of teens' relaxed schedule during the summer. Plan service projects. Stuff bulletins. Do evangelism. Take walks. Clean the church.
- Do youth camp. Trust me.

Youth T

Ask a student to design a T-shirt with the youth group name on it.

Youth on the Web

Invite a teen to create a Web site for the church youth group. Link it to the church Web site, and use tons of photos of every event. Keep it updated because youth will look at it constantly!

Scholarship

Budget or raise some money to be used for scholarships for youth to attend camp, retreats, or events. Allow students who need scholarships to work a specific number of hours to earn it. For example, they might work six hours for camp fees, do office work at the church, rake the yard for a widow in the church, etc.

Prayer Walk

Take teens to prayer walk around their school campus.

Challenge Them Big

Teens are amazingly and uniquely qualified to impact their world for Christ. Challenge them in big ways. They'll rise to the challenge.

Student Leadership

Have a student leadership team of some sort, allowing the team to lead, set up for events, brainstorm ideas, plan camp and mission trip and events. Give them ownership in the youth ministry.

Let's Get Together

Join with other Christian youth groups in your city or state for an event. The event purpose could be fellowship, evangelism, ministry, or Christian growth. And make it a multicultural event.

Job Interview

Make sure the adult leaders for your youth group are top quality. Not just anyone can lead youth. Expect consistent attendance, personal commitment to Christ, and love for youth.